# Go Away

*Travels With, and Without, my Wife*

Mostly Fun

Les Stanley

Copyright © 2024 by Les Stanley
All rights reserved.

The moral right of the author has been asserted.
All rights reserved. No part of this publication may be reproduced, or transmitted by any person or entity (including Google, Amazon or similar organisations), in any form or by any means electronic or mechanical, including photocopying, recording, scanning or by any information storage and retrieval system or transmitted in any form, or by any means without the prior written permission without prior permission in writing from the publisher.

A catalogue record for this book is available from the National Library of Australia.

**Ebook – Kindle**

978-1-7635100-1-2

**Paperback**

978-1-7635100-0-5

Cover Design by nabinkarna on Fiverr
Photo on front cover taken on a tram in Istanbul by author's wife
Photo on back cover taken just waiting for a train at Taormina station, Sicily

www.lesstanley.com

# Contents

| | |
|---|---|
| Foreword by Jeff Stoward | 1 |
| A Word About the Words | 3 |

**Part One**

| | |
|---|---|
| The Plan | 7 |
| Medical Checks | 11 |

**Part Two**

| | |
|---|---|
| To Thailand | 19 |
| Bangkok Nights | 21 |

**Part Three**

| | |
|---|---|
| Istanbul Turkey, via Dubai | 27 |
| Plumbing Problems | 29 |
| The Breakfast Challenge | 33 |
| No Longer Alone | 35 |
| A Tale of Two Topkapis | 41 |
| Am I in Europe or Asia? | 45 |
| I Need to Spend a Lira | 49 |
| A Close Shave | 52 |
| Alone in Istanbul | 56 |
| In Search of the Lost Café | 59 |

**Part Four**

| | |
|---|---|
| To Bucharest, Romania | 63 |
| I Heart Bucharest | 69 |
| A Visit to Ceaușescu's Folly | 71 |
| A Stroll to the Station | 75 |
| The Castle is Closed | 79 |
| Buildings of Sinaia | 81 |
| Sibiu, Romania | 85 |

| | |
|---|---|
| Follow Me, Follow You | 87 |
| Sighișoara, Romania - Dracula's Bedroom | 90 |
| The Cluj Malady | 93 |
| To Oradea, Romania | 96 |
| Across the Border to Hungary | 99 |
| Hungarian Lungs | 100 |
| A Meeting with an Unusual German | 102 |
| In Linz, Austria | 107 |
| The Surprise Astronomer | 109 |
| To Stuttgart, Germany | 112 |
| The 20 Year Construction Project | 114 |
| Lost in Montmartre | 118 |
| The Smallest Restaurant in the World | 122 |
| Safety First | 126 |
| The Still Approaching Storm | 130 |
| He Who is Tired of London | 133 |
| Bring your Own Blue Plaque | 136 |
| Crossing Paris, Heading South | 139 |
| Antibes, France | 144 |
| French Service | 147 |
| The Blue Story | 150 |
| Not Far Now, Sir | 152 |
| Who Wants to Live Forever? | 155 |
| Still on the Tracks | 158 |
| Puccini Lays Down a Tune | 162 |
| I Was Lying in Bed | 166 |
| Rain Falling on my Shoes | 170 |
| Heading Out for the East Coast | 173 |
| A Place to Call my Own | 179 |
| Italian Service | 183 |
| Everybody Back on the Bus | 187 |
| Crossing the Strait of Messina | 191 |
| The Hills of Sicily | 193 |
| Back North to Naples | 197 |
| Day Trips to Sorrento and Pompei | 200 |
| Rome Again | 204 |

## Part Five

| | |
|---|---|
| Back to Bangkok | 209 |
| An Early Morning Call | 213 |
| COVID for Christmas | 218 |
| Undiscovered Bangkok | 221 |
| A Day of Living Dangerously | 223 |
| In On Nut | 237 |
| Out of the City for a Day | 240 |
| Bangkok Smiles | 242 |
| A Positive Day | 243 |
| Time to Go | 246 |
| Isn't it Nice to be Home Again? | 249 |
| | |
| About the Author | 255 |
| Mostly Fun: Soft Nut Bike Tours of Laos and Thailand | 257 |
| Cannes Encore! Travel in the Time of COVID | 259 |
| Soft Nut Bike Tour of Burma | 261 |
| My Brother's Bicycle | 263 |
| Go Away Photos | 265 |

# Foreword by Jeff Stoward

When the British explorers Hume and Hovell, climbed a mountain in 1824 in the southern reaches of what was then New South Wales, they hoped to view Port Phillip Bay in the distance. Unfortunately, the mountain's dense vegetation prevented them from reaching the summit, resulting in immense disappointment. In addition, Hume suffered a painful injury to his groin on the trip which caused him much distress and necessitated a five-day rest.

Reading Les Stanley's latest epic, "Go Away", I was struck by the similarities Les shared with these two unfortunates, who went on to name that place "Mt Disappointment", and not just because of groin injuries. Les takes disappointment to the next level. More than disappointed, he's often annoyed; by surly waiters and extortionate entry fees, among other things. Certain places escape his easily activated wrath; he loves Romania and Italy, most of the time. And Bangkok, well who couldn't be happy in Bangkok? This may not sound like a positive plug for his book, but stick with me, as I explain just why it is so.

You might be aware of the German word *Schadenfreude* - that pleasure derived by someone (in this case the reader), observing another person's misfortune (in this case the author). How much enjoyment I got out of reading about the problems Les encounters I won't share, because I'm not in the business of making myself look bad in public. But you can, in the privacy of your own home, laugh at Les, as he is tormented by rude and/or aggressive service staff, loud and inconsiderate fellow travellers, and revel in his discomfort generally as he takes flight across Asia and Europe on his latest adventure.

The thing is, we've all been there. We've all suffered at the behaviour of others; it's just that Les focuses our attention on the banality and overall discomfort of 'travel'....and yet we yearn for it, and can't wait to do it all again. To suffer disappointment, when we were expecting something more. Like life really.

Enjoy reading "Go Away" and feel free to laugh at Les as you do.

Jeff Stoward, Author of European Nonsense. www.jeffstoward.com

# A Word About the Words

As I was born in the UK in the 50s and have lived in Australia, on and off, since 1989, I'm blessed with being bi-calibrate, i.e., able to think in both metric and imperial measures. Some readers of this book may not be so lucky. I've used metric measurements when describing distances and temperatures.

It's easy enough to convert from metric to imperial if you need to; 8 kilometres equals 5 miles or, a kilometre is around 60% of a mile.

With temperatures, to get it exactly right you'd divide by 5, multiply by 9 and then add 32! A simpler way, though not 100% accurate is to double the centigrade or Celsius temperature and add 30.

. . .

No need to worry too much about temperatures affecting your enjoyment of the book. I've only mentioned them in Thailand, so just assume, whatever the number, it's hot.

Regarding spelling I've used standard UK English spelling throughout. If that irks you just do your own translation; in words such as realise and organise, *s* equals *z*. Most words containing *our* use an extra *u*, except *our* of c*our*se, that would be silly.

I've mostly avoided using the real names of family and friends and referred to them by their first initial. One character, T, crops up frequently. This is my short suffering wife, Tracy.

# Part One

# The Plan

Less than a month after returning from my previous trip, hilariously chronicled in, *Mostly Fun - Soft Nut Bike Tours of Laos and Thailand*, I started planning my next adventure. I was reminded of a comment a colleague had made when I greeted him at work one Monday morning.

-*Good weekend?* I asked.

-*Already planning the next one*, he rakishly responded.

The title of this book, *Go Away*, came to me one afternoon, around half-way through the trip, during one of the periods when T had joined me. Go away might at first sound like a negative response to no longer being alone on my travels. Not so, it was a reaction to the frequency with which other travellers, and in some cases, local people, annoyed me with their habits and customs. It also perfectly described my constant state of *Fernweh* – a strong desire to be somewhere else.

. . .

To put the grand plan together I spent weeks searching on *Skyscanner, Airbnb* and *Booking.com* for flights and accommodation. I also delved deep into the vast amount of information available on *Seat61.com*, along with investigating options on different European train websites. I needed two plans, as I had to take into account the fact T was now working, and was therefore restricted as to when she could travel. I mapped out a route that would allow us to meet up when she had vacation time. The main factors in the plan were; T wanted to visit Taormina in Italy as she had based a recent novel there, and I had long harboured a desire to go to Romania and Hungary. Also, we both agreed Turkey looked interesting.

The plan in brief was as follows; first, I'd fly to Bangkok, revisit some old haunts and break the journey to Europe. Then another flight, on to Istanbul, Turkey. A month or so later, once her vacation time began, T could join me in Istanbul. We looked at options to visit other parts of Turkey, but eventually agreed to find a good place to stay in the city and explore its environs.

Once T flew home to return to work, I would set off on the European part of my odyssey. My original intention was to travel by train across Western Turkey and Bulgaria into Romania and then continue, always by train, all the way to London. But when I found a low-cost carrier operating between Istanbul and Bucharest, I was happy to take that option and cut back a bit on travel by rail. A

Romanian friend offered some advice on towns to visit as I made my way across the country. From the Romania/Hungary border I would follow a relatively straight line, north-west across central Europe; through Hungary, Austria, Germany and France en route to the UK. After dodging the rain in England I intended to cross France again and meet up with T in Rome, after which we would travel south, via Naples to Sicily. The penultimate stage was to be a flight together from Rome to Bangkok. At journey's end, we'd spend Christmas in Vietnam and finally fly back home to Brisbane, with a week in Bangkok for any last-minute shopping. I'd be away for a total of four months.

Of the many writers who have inspired me over the years, one must be Paul Theroux. The journey he undertook to write his genre-defining travel book, *The Great Railway Bazaar* also took four months.

Never writing a particularly positive account of the countries he passes through, or the people he meets, towards the end of the book Theroux becomes even more curmudgeonly. This is mainly because he is missing his wife and the comfort of home. Desperate to make it home for Christmas, he struggles with flight, ship and train cancellations caused by bad weather.

The last chapters of Theroux's book could have been an inspiration for the hilarious Steve Martin/John Candy film; *Trains, Planes and Automobiles*.

. . .

I know how he felt. Not that I wanted to be home for Christmas but I would rather not have spent it suffering a mild dose of COVID in Vietnam. There's no denying that four months is a long time to be away.

It wasn't all bad though. Far from it. I loved the people and sights of Romania. I learnt much about the history of Paris thanks to two days spent, in the rain, with a friend who lives there and is a passionate and knowledgeable history teacher. Italy was a feast of pizza and wine with some historical marvels thrown in. Bangkok, as ever, was *mostly fun*.

# Medical Checks

I had a few health scares in the months prior to my departure. Like all good hypochondriacs, I kept a diary, or timeline, of my ailments.

Six months before leaving, a nagging pain in my groin persuaded me to have an ultrasound and a hernia was discovered. I'd been vaguely aware that something was wrong when I was on the bike trips described in *Mostly Fun – Soft Nut Bike Tours in Laos and Thailand*.

While recuperating from the hernia surgery, my exercise regime was severely restricted. This led to my back strain reoccurring. I was leaning forward to pick up my trousers one morning and felt a sharp twinge in the lower lumbar region. This incapacitated me for a while.

. . .

Then, around six weeks before I was planning to board a plane and jet off for four months, a routine visit to the doctor, and a brief conversation about my family history, led to me having a CT scan on my heart. The scan revealed a partial blockage in one artery. I learned that, whilst there are four chambers in the heart, there are only three arteries. This means that the left side of the heart, is fed by one single artery - the left ventricle artery, known in the trade as the LVA. A design fault, if ever there was one. The blockage in this artery meant that, should it become worse, I could have a severe heart attack. Yikes! The doctor calmly explained all this, while I sat numbly watching my travel plans fly out of his office window. He added that it was likely I would need a stent inserted and to start taking blood thinners. In the 10 seconds he took to tell me this I felt my age increase by 10 years. A week later I was subjected to an angiogram. Fortunately, the angiogram revealed that the blockage was less serious than first thought.

*-No blood thinners. No stent. Come back and see me in two years,* said the affable doctor.


Less than two weeks before I was due to leave, a sore tooth forced me to visit the dentist, where it was confirmed that a crown was needed. Originally the dentist told me that it took three weeks to complete the procedure. When I explained my travel plans, she said it could be done more quickly at extra cost. Used to haggling, though not for dental work, I was successful in arranging for the crown to be completed in time and not to pay the additional cost.

. . .

## Medical Checks

As the date of departure came closer, I began, as usual, to feel restless. I'd begun organising things way ahead of time, too far probably, and had by now booked all the flights, accommodation and trains that were needed. I'd also packed my small suitcase, adding bits and pieces as I thought of them, I remembered I'd done this once before, for a business trip and then arrived at my destination, ready to run a training course for an important customer, but without any business shirts.

But it wasn't over yet. Over the weekend, 10 days before I was due to fly out, I could feel a small dent of some kind in my abdomen. In fact, I'd had this for a while, since surgery for prostate cancer some 10 years previously. It was related to scar tissue. But now, I could swear, the dent, dip, hole, whatever the hell it was, was getting bigger. Another visit to the doctor was called for. She assured me it was probably nothing but sent me for an ultrasound scan anyway. The ultrasound lady was very thorough and poked and prodded deeply with her apparatus. I knew from past experience that normally, they wouldn't reveal any details and will tell you to talk to your doctor. But I felt happy when, as I was standing with my trousers round my ankles, wiping the gel off, she casually asked me where I was going. When I replied,

-*Asia and Europe,* adding, *hopefully,* she simply said,

-*You should be fine.* A positive omen, if ever there was one.

This just left me with the tooth situation. I called in to the dentist's surgery a day or two before departure, but my crown had still not arrived.

*-I guess they don't send them by post,* I said, *surely you can check with the courier company?*

But the best they could offer was that, if necessary, the dentist could work on Saturday, which was apparently her daughter's birthday. I was due to leave the following Tuesday. All I could do was wait.

Far more stressful than the health situation was the fact that I had by now watched, or more correctly re-watched, for at least the third or fourth time, all available *Star Trek, The Next Generation,* episodes. How would I spend my afternoons without the distraction of Worf's stoicism, Riker's dedication to duty and Picard's exemplary leadership skills? Not to mention my internal debate as to whether, in that fantasy life we all have, Doctor Crusher or Counsellor Troy would have been my girlfriend. Further adding to my mental strife, was that, the latest iteration of the franchise, *Brave New Worlds* had, temporarily I could only hope, also finished. Compared to this, my medical problems paled into insignificance.

Despite all this, I tried, as always, to be positive. I'd recently discovered that there are two types of stress. Negative stress, or distress, which I think we're all familiar with. There's also eustress, or positive stress. I focused on the benefits of the past weeks or so and was convinced the stress had, at least in part, been a good thing. I had not felt like eating so much and that, combined with my resolve to stop drinking, had helped me lose five kilos.

However, in the next couple of days the situation, again, took a turn for the worse. I'd bounced back after the lady at the ultrasound scan had told me, or at least implied, all was well. In fact, I'd felt so positive, I'd even regained my appetite and had a burger for lunch. But when I went to the doctor the next day, to receive details of the scan, it turned out that I did indeed have another hernia. This bought my total lifetime hernia score up to four, surely some kind of record. It was not what I had expected, or wanted to hear.

I consoled myself with the fact that, two doctors, one a surgeon, who was familiar with my medical history, had told me that despite my situation, it was fine to wait a few months for surgery and that travelling overseas involved minimal risk.

So, I decided to *Go Away*.

# Part Two

# To Thailand

T dropped me at Brisbane airport on her way to work. I'd be seeing her again in Istanbul in two weeks.

I'd already checked in online for my morning flight to Bangkok. But I still had to drop my bag off. At many airports, including Brisbane, the process is completely automated these days. People complain about self-service checkouts at supermarkets, but you haven't experienced anything, if you haven't done your own bag drop. Scanned and tagged I watched my small suitcase disappear into the bowels of the airport. In the departure area, after indulging in an overpriced coffee, I searched, as I had on many previous occasions, for somewhere comfortable and quiet to wait. But the airport design still only seemed to cater for beings that were twice the size of a normal human. I idly wondered if these same designers were the ones who calculated the maximum occupancy of an elevator. Where I live, this is defined as 14 people or

1050 kilos. In reality you'd be hard pressed, to accommodate more than eight.

Eventually, as I had done on previous occasions, I made my way to an empty gate where there were some normal seats.

My flights were full of other excited travellers, but bearable. I was pleased that the person in front of me did not recline their seat. I had some trouble with the connector of my headphones and ended up watching a couple of movies, with subtitles in English, to follow what was going on. After a while, I realised that this meant I could watch the movie and listen to some podcasts I had downloaded, at the same time. Quite a feast for the senses.

Arriving in Bangkok I took the train into the city. I'd done this many times before and it always gave me a slight thrill, feeling I was as close to being a local as I would ever be. I tried taking a short cut from the station to where my accommodation was. Even though I had lived on this same street for three years, I managed to get lost.

# Bangkok Nights

My Bangkok plans were simple. Meet up with a few old friends, get a haircut and maybe a massage or two. As I'd lived in the city for eight years, I had no intention of doing any sightseeing. In any case I'd be stopping there again on the way home with T. Sightseeing and other activities could wait until then.

I slept fitfully on my first night and was, as expected, wide awake at 03:00am. I was staying in Nana, the entertainment area of the city. I was well aware that, If I'd stepped out of the door of the apartment, I could certainly have found something to do. But I wasn't in the mood for pleasures of the flesh. I read for a bit and monastically waited for day to break. Around 06:30am, still too early, for much that would interest me to be open, even in Thailand, I crawled out of bed. I made my way to a restaurant I liked, hoping to get breakfast. But it wasn't open, and I wandered aimlessly for a while among the detritus of the previous night, until another food place nearby opened its doors at 07:00am.

My second night in Bangkok ended in another early morning which found me wide awake well before dawn. I'm sure it's an age thing. I seldom have an issue going to sleep, but staying asleep was not so easy. It was an expected pattern taking the three-hour time difference in to account and I awoke around 04:00am. Once it got light, I went for a walk towards the park, planning to get a cannabis coffee from the vending machine I'd discovered on a previous visit. I fed my coins into the brightly coloured machine and, full of anticipation, pushed the relevant button. The machine sprang into life and played a little tune while I waited expectantly. But when I retrieved the cup from its small compartment, I was disappointed to find it contained only warm water. No coffee and presumably, no cannabis.

Later in the day, I arranged to meet some of my old Bangkok workmates for lunch. The company I used to work for had recently relocated and I was keen to see the new office. It was all very hi-tech, with card reading lifts and vending machines for food and drink scattered everywhere. We walked to a nearby restaurant and I listened to their tales of work-related shenanigans. Nothing much seemed to have changed in the eight years since I had moved on.

. . .

September is still the rainy season in Bangkok and true to form it rained intermittently all day. I spent most of the afternoon laying on the bed watching videos on YouTube, occasionally venturing outside for food. Not exactly a productive day. In the evening, I had arranged to meet one of the members of the cycling group mentioned in *Mostly Fun*. We had dinner in a nearby hotel and he promised to buy a copy of the book. I was a little concerned about this, as I had described him somewhat negatively in my retelling of our cycling trip through Laos. He kept his word and was obviously a quick reader, as, a day later, I received a message from him saying he was sorry we hadn't hit it off when we first met.

After three days I finally had a reasonably good night's sleep, despite the sound of furniture moving in the apartment above. My body clock had reset itself and I slept through to 06:00am. It wasn't raining and, eager to get some exercise, I set off for my morning stroll, passing the coffee vending machine but, not wishing to waste 40 baht again on a cup of hot water, I did not partake. A little later I passed a human coffee maker who had an extensive list of beverages for sale. I ordered a cappuccino. When I received it, I realised that her marketing ploy was to advertise all sorts of caffeine-based concoctions, but in reality, to only make one thing, strong sweet coffee. I drank it anyway.

That evening, I met up with another group of ex-work colleagues. One of them had just returned from a business trip to Israel and I tried to impress her with my knowledge of the country and the language. She politely feigned interest for a while, but I could tell she didn't really want to know what I had been up to there, 50 years ago. Before meeting them for dinner, I had, earlier in the day, made the trip to the assigned restaurant so that I would not have trouble finding it later. The restaurant where we had arranged to meet was in one of the many *sois* or small streets off Sukhumvit. I took the BTS to Phrom Phong before walking along the *soi* to where we were to meet. I was beginning to hate Sukhumvit Road. It was always so noisy and crowded. I also wondered why the BTS only ever has one escalator at each station, and why it was seldom on the side that I was using. Cost explained the first part of this conundrum, but not the second.

The social whirl continued with me meeting another friend for lunch. We arranged to meet in Terminal 21, a well-known shopping centre in the Asoke area of the city. After a very pleasant Japanese meal, we wandered around for a while in the air conditioning, chatting about our lives. I was still impressing myself by avoiding alcohol. I'd started this abstemious regime after the heart scare, even though the doctor told me that the heart wasn't greatly affected by moderate alcohol intake. I wasn't sure how my resolve would work out once I reached Turkey where, according to my pre-trip research, beer should be very cheap.

# Part Three

# Istanbul Turkey, via Dubai

The day came to leave Bangkok. A city where I knew my way around and, perhaps more importantly, knew how things worked; the transport system, the best places to get coffee and to eat. Part of me was excited by the challenge of going to a new place. Not strictly new, as I had stopped off in Istanbul many years previously, on my way to India. Back then I'd spent the night on the train from Sofia, Bulgaria. I'd befriended an American chain-smoker on the train. We'd arrived in Istanbul and, to keep costs down, shared a room for a few nights. My abiding memory of him was that, each night after fastidiously cleaning his teeth in the bathroom attached to our small room, the first thing he did was to light up another cigarette.

Back in the present day, getting to Istanbul meant a day on planes. My flight from Bangkok to Dubai was uneventful and I had a fair bit of room. Connecting in the cavernous halls of Dubai International was something else I had done many times and it presented no problem. Dubai airport was very peaceful, as airports go, they don't make constant boarding announcements any more. Other airports should try this. My onward flight from Dubai to Istanbul was less enjoyable. A large group of South Americans were boarding. Nobody seemed to understand the concept of seat numbers and there was a lot of confused shouting in Spanish. Eventually everyone found their seat, the doors were closed and we rattled down the runway. I guessed the group had come off a long flight as the lady next to me kept falling asleep on my shoulder. Dubai to Istanbul was a fairly short flight, around five hours, so I bore her intrusion into my personal space stoically.

We landed in Istanbul and the South Americans headed off, no doubt, on a guided tour. The new airport, called Istanbul Grand Airport, opened in 2019. It was very sparkly and obviously built for future expansion. Much walking was involved; from gate to immigration, immigration to baggage, baggage to arrivals hall. I bought a SIM for my phone, which on reflection was expensive. A sign of things to come. There was a train from the airport into the city but, it was late and I was tired so I sought out the taxi queue and took a taxi into town, vainly trying to recognise anything from almost 50 years previously.

# Plumbing Problems

For the three weeks I would be in Istanbul, most of which would be with T, I'd selected a classy looking apartment in an area called Beyoğlu. Classy looking on the Airbnb website at least. My expectations weren't high as the taxi I'd taken from the airport pulled up in a narrow lane, beside an ancient looking building. The owner, who lived elsewhere, had given me the name of his neighbour as a contact and she was there to meet me. I made my way inside, up some of the steepest steps I had ever encountered. Once inside, the apartment seemed to live up to the description of its owner and the reviews of others who had stayed there. It was spacious and bright. I unpacked a few things and tried to take a shower. There was no hot water. At first, I thought I just had to wait a while for it to run through. I was used to this, coming from England. A country where bathing is not a high priority and hot, high-pressure showers, are still, almost unheard of. No matter how long I waited, the water remained tepid. I showered anyway, thinking I was lucky not to be using a bucket. Then I contacted the owner.

He apologised profusely and gave me some instructions regarding taps and levers in a cupboard in the bedroom. I'd already found the hot water tank there, and checked that it was switched on. But this Byzantian system was different. It required knowledge of plumbing that only an expert would possess. I crawled around in the cupboard, timidly pulling at levers and pressing buttons, while the host gave me instructions via WhatsApp, to no avail. He promised to send someone in the morning. The next day there was a ring on the door bell. A friendly chap in overalls, carrying a large spanner entered, and headed straight for the bedroom where the water tank cupboard was situated. I had the distinct feeling he had been there before. I followed him and observed him turning the same lever I had tried to turn the previous night. The only difference was that he was turning it in the opposite direction. I heard the faint gurgling sound of water running into the tank. He turned to me and said something in Turkish which I didn't understand. He held up three fingers and pointed to the lever. This helped a bit but I was still confused. Finally, in exasperation he fumbled in the voluminous pockets of his stained overalls and produced a phone. He spoke into it in Turkish before proffering the device in my direction. On the screen, below whatever he had said in Turkish, was written,
   *-Turn every three days.*

. . .

Then he confused me again, holding up all his fingers before again speaking into the phone. The translation this time was.
 -*Only ten minutes.*

He heaved his bulk back into the cupboard and turned the lever again, in the opposite direction. Turning back to me he triumphantly announced, in English,
 -*OK!*

On that positive note, still carrying the spanner he had not used, he left the building. I surmised that him carrying a spanner was akin to the way, during my working life, I would always ensure I carried a file, or sheet of paper, with me when, simply to alleviate the boredom, I took unnecessary walks around whichever dull office I was working in. It was proof of his trade and confirmation, should anyone be observing him, that he was not simply wandering the streets.

To be certain I had properly understood the plumber's brief instructions, I contacted the apartment owner. He confirmed that the lever turning must be done every three days. He also confirmed the importance of only turning on the flow for 10 minutes saying,
 -*Turkish plumbing, very old.*

The next day I ventured out in search of sustenance. I had some greasy bread and a Turkish coffee at a bakery near the apartment. On the way back I passed a couple of much better-looking places. One had a large sign above its welcoming doors which simply said, in English - *Breakfast*. I promised myself I'd go there the following day.

Later that day I attempted to find my way to the airport by public transport. This was in preparation to meet T, who would be arriving the following evening. It wasn't easy getting to the airport and involved a number of changes. My first attempt at negotiating the Istanbul Metro system was a failure and I gave up. Later the same day I tried again. This time, instead of using the Metro, I took a taxi to the station from where the dedicated airport train departed. This proved more successful. The taxi ride was not pleasant though. The driver took a circuitous route and I arrived at Kâğıthane station feeling nauseous. I explored the station for a while, then headed home, confident I would be able to find my way the next day.

# The Breakfast Challenge

I continued looking for a supermarket that sold more than chocolate and cigarettes. I was missing Bangkok's ubiquitous 7-Elevens. I tried to get breakfast at the place nearby I'd seen the day before. Once again, they sold a variety of greasy looking bread, but after the previous day's experience, I was wise to the inedibility of this and chose something else. It turned out to be a kind of dry pastry, filled with jam. Almost equally unpleasant. I was excited by the large sign saying coffee, and requested a cup, but the owner simply replied,

-*Coffee, no.*

I tried another place, run by a young guy who spoke good English. I regretted my choice when he switched on the music, but I'd already taken a seat. However, when I asked for coffee, he said it would take 10 minutes for his machine to warm up, so I pretended I was in a hurry and used this as an excuse to leave.

. . .

Later in the day I made my way to the airport to meet T. Better prepared this time, I easily negotiated the complicated changes, despite the fact that I was travelling in the rush hour. On board the airport train I became confused as I looked at the route map. It showed two stops, both of which may have been my desired destination. One was simply named, *Terminal 2*. The other, *Istanbul Havalimani*. Terminal 2 turned out to be an unopened station, being built for future expansion. The other, *Havalimani* was the Turkish word for airport. Like many things, simple once you know, but stressful when you don't.

I purchased another *Istanbulkart* on arrival at the airport. This local travel card is indispensable for anyone visiting the city and allows transport on all trains, buses, trams and ferries. If only they would make it a little easier to buy. The machines that dispense the cards must have been created in the early days of computer technology and featured touch screens that barely worked. After much stabbing at various buttons, I managed to complete my purchase. Then came the additional task of topping the card up. It came with no value on it. Most notes pushed into the relevant slot were immediately rejected. But I persevered and came away with a card that T could hopefully use.

# No Longer Alone

Back in the apartment the hot water stopped working again. But this time I knew what to do and soon had it pumping out steaming, scalding water. However, I failed to turn the magic lever off in time and we had a small flood. Luckily, we were close to Mount Ararat.

The next morning, we continued our search for a supermarket, eventually finding a local branch of Carrefour. After stocking up with essential purchases we wandered together down Istiklal, one of the main thoroughfares of Istanbul. Occasionally we stopped to try and casually peruse a restaurant menu. This was difficult as, each time we approached an establishment, an overzealous employee would stand within inches of our faces, imploring us to enter. This aggressive behaviour had the opposite of the desired effect and we would leave.

. . .

In the afternoon we made our way to the main tourist hub of the city, the Sultanahmet area. Many of the city's main attractions are located in this part of town; The Blue Mosque, Hagia Sophia mosque and Topkapi Palace to name but a few. T was keen to visit the nearby Grand Bazaar. I was less enthusiastic, but I'd made a pact with myself to go along, uncomplainingly, with any activities she proposed.

We squeezed into a crowded tram and bumped and swayed our way to the relevant stop. Alighting from the tram we were swept into the melee and entered the bazaar. It was disappointing to say the least. Now nothing more than a sanitised version of what must have been. Most shops sold fake Gucci T-shirts or other useless tat. After mooching around the area for a few more minutes, we took the tram back in the direction of the harbour, passing the main train station and the famous Pudding Shop, all of which would have been in the area where I stayed when I visited in my past life, more than 40 years previously.

The Pudding Shop, officially Lale Restaurant has a special place in the hearts and minds of anyone who travelled the fabled *Hippy Trail* between Europe and Kathmandu in the 60s and 70s. Situated almost directly opposite Istanbul's main station, this small restaurant was opened by brothers Idris and Namık Çolpan. Before the advent of email, messaging and the other numerous communication systems that came later, it was the place to meet fellow, intrepid travellers on the road East. Here, one could pick up a lift to Eastern Turkey and on to Iran, buy, or sell, a van or truck which had been used to complete the Europe to Delhi overland route, or just get the name of the cheapest place to stay in Herat or Kabul.

It was still a great place for a drink or a simple meal and a good spot to people watch. Many passersby were tourists but, sit long enough, waiting for your coffee to cool and you'd also see plenty of locals. Most Turkish women wear conservative clothes. Either the full *yashmak* where all one can see is a pair of beady eyes, or a loose fitting, grey or black, tent like dress. There were a few exceptions and one morning we spotted a young lady, probably in her early 20s, sporting a tight fitting, shimmering pair of what I can only describe as hot-pants. Her tiny Turkish buttocks quivered beneath the shiny, figure-hugging material. Goodness knows what the tent ladies who saw her must have thought.

Slowly but surely the Istanbul transportation system was beginning to make sense. Today we discovered that, instead of stumbling down a very steep hill to the nearest tram stop, which meant staggering up that same hill at the end of our day's activities, we could take another train from a station much nearer our accommodation, one stop, to connect with the tram. We wandered around the Sultanahmet area trying to find a restaurant which met our needs. These were simple; acceptable food and a pleasant ambience. As always, any approach to a likely looking place, meant being immediately accosted by the aggressive owner, or his frequently more aggressive staff.

We eventually succumbed to the constant cajoling and took a table at a place where we were told we would get a 20% discount. After eating, this proved true, after we reminded them of the promise, and I could not have been happier.

We were staying quite close to Istiklal Avenue, one of Istanbul's most well-known areas. There was something happening on the avenue today. Police were everywhere, armed with guns and carrying riot shields. We ventured out in search of coffee and when I asked the bearded, tobacco reeking, café owner what was happening he replied, mysteriously,
  -*An event*.

Later in the day, having survived *the event* we headed for another part of town where we again, struggled to find somewhere to eat. Not that there aren't plenty of restaurants in this city, even if their menus tend to all be pretty much the same. We chose a place near the water and settled down for a drink and to peruse the menu. The owner spotted us checking reviews, which were mostly negative, and insisted that he had bought the restaurant only two weeks previously. We had planned to eat but his incessant talk proved too much for me and we left after finishing our drinks. Asking for the bill confused our young waiter who reappeared with two more beers which we politely declined.

. . .

Our second choice, if it can be called that, seemed fine until we looked at the menu. Everything was at least twice as expensive as we had paid the previous night. After a short, heated discussion with the manager, I was charged A$5 for a bottle of water I had not ordered and we escaped. In the end we went back to the place we had gone to the previous evening. Haggling hard, we negotiated the same 20% discount that had been offered the day before. Finally feeling relaxed, away from the madness, we enjoyed dinner.

We found another new route home. The aptly named Tünel, an underground train running between Karaköy and Beyoğlu. The Tünel is an historic, underground, rubber-tyred funicular line. It has two stations, connecting Karaköy and Beyoğlu, which is at one end of Istiklal. The tunnel runs uphill from near the confluence of the Golden Horn with the Bosphorus and is about 573 metres (1,880 feet) long. It was opened on 17 January, 1875. It's the second-oldest fully underground urban railway in the world. The London Underground is the oldest, having its origins in the Metropolitan Railway which opened on 10 January 1863.

We realised, on arrival at Beyoğlu station at one end of Istiklal, that we had passed the entrance on our long walk, a day earlier, down the hill in search of The Galata Tower. As there was an entrance fee of A$30 to the tower, and a lengthy queue, like many of the famous city sites, we gave it a miss.

. . .

Wandering the streets was an interesting way to spend our days, but when the time came to take a relaxing break and get a coffee, it could be trying. One day we spotted a cosy nice-looking place and went inside. We found a table and took a seat. Three waiters wandered around, studiously ignoring us. After a couple of minutes of this I said, perhaps a little too loudly, to the one I had almost bumped into on entering,
 -*Excuse me, hello.*


He looked uninterestedly in my direction. I asked for a menu and he pointed to a tiny QR code taped to one of the many ashtrays, mumbling something incoherent. I sighed and tried to get my phone to read it. It couldn't. We left.

# A Tale of Two Topkapis

Having so far avoided the main Istanbul sights for a variety of reasons; cost, heat, long queues, we decided today would be the day we would at least tackle the Topkapi Palace.

Wikipedia gives the following concise description:
*The Topkapı Palace is a large museum and library in the east of the Fatih district of Istanbul in Turkey. From the 1460s to the completion of Dolmabahçe Palace in 1856, it served as the administrative centre of the Ottoman Empire, and was the main residence of its sultans.*

A friend of ours from Brisbane, who by coincidence was also spending time in Istanbul, had told us that the various famous mosques were nothing special. This was mainly because, even though they looked spectacular from the outside, they were quite dull inside. Knowing that Islam seems, to the outsider at least, to be a religion which pretty much bans the having of fun, this did not surprise me. I was loath to buy tickets online beforehand, convinced that this would mean paying more. We set off on the tram in the direction of Topkapi. As we sat on the tram, rolling and tumbling along, we both commented that it seemed odd that it was so far out of town and that there were. very few tourists heading to it. On arrival we realised why. Although there is a tram stop called Topkapi, which, one could reasonably assume, was where the palace of the same name might be situated, this turned out not to be the case. We'd gone to Topkapi park by mistake. It was a pleasant enough spot but not the destination we had in mind. Reboarding the tram, we noticed that, on the route map, in fine print next to the well-known stop Sultanahmet, was also written, Topkapi Palace.

We made our way into the grounds of the famous edifice; this at least was free. Then we spotted the ticket office for entrance to the palace itself. An interesting ploy was in evidence here. Emblazoned in large print were two entry prices; 950TL (Turkish Lira) for a pass to the palace and two mosques which were anyway free to enter, and a price for entry just to the palace itself, 750TL. The Turkish economy had been experiencing rampant inflation for some years and these prices equated to around A$60 and A$50 respectively. In tiny print just beneath these was the price for Turkish citizens of 150TL and 100TL. I'd come across this scourge of dual pricing before in Thailand. There, they cunningly write the amount, using the otherwise seldom used, Thai number characters, assuming that ignorant foreigners will not notice.

## A Tale of Two Topkapis

There's an argument, of course, for dual pricing in that locals should have cheaper access to their own heritage. Also, that they pay taxes and perhaps, although I think this is unlikely, some part of that goes towards the upkeep of these places. But imagine trying something like this in Europe or Australia? You'd be accused of racism.

I was happy to take this blatant attempt at daylight robbery, as an omen that we were not destined to visit what was, despite its historical significance, now little more than one more tourist trap. I wasn't concerned. Perhaps I wasn't Ranulph Fiennes, Chris Bonnington or Edmund Hilary but I'd trekked to Everest Base Camp. I'd seen the Taj Mahal, twice. I'd visited The Potala Palace in Lhasa, Tibet. Cruised the backwaters of Kerala. Sailed on the ferry from Rameswarem, India to Talimanar, Sri Lanka. Travelled by train across the Sydney Harbour Bridge, with its spectacular view of The Opera House. Commuted, on foot, across Hyde Park, along Park Lane and down Oxford Street in London. Swum, or at least floated, in the Dead Sea. I'd ridden a camel around the Pyramids at Giza. Driven along the lower, middle and upper corniches of the French Riviera. I once slept in the grounds of The Acropolis. The list goes on. Even though I've never crossed the Rubicon, or, as yet, sailed on the river Styx, I had definitely reached a stage in my life, where ancient buildings, or places on other peoples' bucket list, didn't interest me.

We went to have a coffee in the Topkapi gift shop and admire the view. The coffee was overpriced. It was also disgusting. After a few sips we both agreed it was undrinkable and left. We wandered through more markets and eventually, to my delight and T's disappointment, emerged near The Pudding Shop. Here we had a delicious Turkish coffee and Baklava. As we consumed our refreshments, I sat quietly contemplating the dubious glories of my past.

# Am I in Europe or Asia?

I noticed, eavesdropping on fellow tourist's conversations, that people seem very confused as to whether they are on the European or the Asian side of Istanbul. In reality it makes little difference, but I guess it's fun to know as Istanbul is the only city in the world which spans two continents. The confusion stems from the ubiquity of water and the fact that when travelling from one tourist area to another, you often traverse a bridge over water. But this bridge is not the one that spans the two continents. The crossing that confuses the uneducated masses, is usually the Galata bridge, which simply connects two separate areas on the European side of the city. We crossed this bridge many times, usually on the tram, occasionally on foot, and frequently heard people saying they were excited to be crossing from Europe to Asia. Excited they may have been, but crossing continents they were not.

. . .

Today we discovered more about the, at first, apparently very practical *IstanbulKart*. We'd become used to top-up machines that didn't work. We assumed that they were rejecting our various Turkish Lira notes because they were crumpled, or damaged in some other way. Or that we were putting them in the machine upside down. But, as we were struggling, yet again with loading money onto our card, a friendly local explained the situation.

-*You can only put 500 Lira a month,* he said.


That was it. It explained why, once or twice when we had tried loading low denomination notes, or a few coins on the card we had been successful. Our new friend explained that residents could buy a different card, which had a much higher limit. But that had to be registered by showing a Turkish ID card. The impracticality of only being able to load 500TL, approximately A$25.00 a month onto the card was obvious. Trips on the Metro and buses were cheap enough, but you only had to take a couple of ferries and you would soon get through 100TL in a day. The only solution, once the limit was reached, was to buy a new card. By the end of our stay, we had a stack of them, all with an unspendable, small denomination remaining. We left them behind, thinking perhaps our Airbnb host might offer them to new tenants, once the month expired and they could be reused. The card is a good idea and makes getting around cheap enough, compared to Europe or Australia. But why, oh why, not make it easier to use?

. . .

Enterprising, but immoral, locals had instigated a simple scam when they spotted yet another tourist struggling with a recalcitrant *IstanbulKart* machine. Near machines in more crowded places, two of them would stand innocently by and, when they spied a frustrated visitor, unsuccessfully trying to purchase, or top-up, their card, they would spring into action, asking if they could help. Should you naïvely hand them the cash you had intended to feed into the machine, some of it would quickly be handed over to scam guy number two, who would disappear into the crowd. By the time you had realised that only 100TL of the 200TL you had intended for the card had actually been added, both petty criminals were long-gone.

Even with an *IstanbulKart*, travelling on the transport system took a bit of getting used to. Stations seldom connected well. It wasn't just that there were long distances to be walked, I was used to that, having used the underground transport systems in many large cities. But, in Istanbul, a connection nearly always involved crossing a major road. Also, the cigarette smoking locals had not quite grasped the concept of letting people off the train before they tried to barge on. Once or twice, when this happened, I would push back, often having no choice but to thrust my pagan body against the nylon clad, shapeless dress of a local female, who seemed desperate to board. This lack of courtesy wasn't restricted to public transport. It happened all the time in any crowded place where, from time to time, tired of constantly changing direction to avoid yet another, phone-gazing local, I would simply keep walking in a straight line until, at the last moment, if I was lucky, they'd look up and change direction.

# I Need to Spend a Lira

Unlike the Metro, the ferries were spacious and easy to board. We went by ferry to the suburb of Ortakoy. This picturesque part of town had been recommended to us as a must see. We worked out which boat to take and sat on the quay waiting for it to dock so that we could board. I took advantage of this time to visit my first Turkish public toilet. I'll spare you the full details. I was keen to experience this, as I had read that the *Istanbulkart* could also be used to access public toilets. This feature of the card intrigued me and I was keen to see how it worked. Very well, thank you and only 1 TL or 5 cents.

I boarded the ferry much relaxed and we headed out along the Bosphorus. The views were wonderful, the air clear and, apart from the dull rhythmic pumping of the engines, quiet. The ferries soon became my preferred mode of transport in Istanbul.

. . .

My phone had been playing up over the previous few days. It kept hanging and not letting me access apps. I deleted everything I didn't need, but it seemed to make no difference. The device was five years old, positively ancient in the world of technology. It was time to buy a new one. I asked about prices in a couple of local shops but where we were staying, in tourist town, everything was 20% or so more than the price I'd seen on the Samsung website.

We took the train out to a major shopping centre in the suburbs and found a Samsung dealer. I went to a few other shops first and they all tried to upsell me to something I did not need. Following the phone purchase two things happened. My other phone started working perfectly well again, and I spent days wandering the streets looking for a case for the new one. Of course, the only thing available in every shop I went into was for new iPhones.

Before departing Australia, just after my heart scare, I had made up my mind to give up, or at least cut back on drinking alcohol. I hadn't found this anywhere near as much of a challenge as I thought I would. On the way back from my first visit to the heart guy, I'd called in to a bar I'd seen many times, but always been driving past, unable to visit. I'd had just one pint and, vowing to myself that would be it, I'd headed home.

. . .

## I Need to Spend a Lira

I'd done well in Turkey and despite having the odd beer, just to be sociable, had not succumbed to getting back into my old habits. This was partly, truth be told, almost wholly, due to the fact that the A$1.50 pints of my favourite Tuborg beer, I'd found whilst searching the internet, did not exist. Rampant inflation meant that beer in a bar was around A$7.50, still cheap compared to Australia, but not the drinkers dream I had envisaged. Also, I had yet to find Tuborg Green anywhere. Turkish drinkers seemed to favour the hitherto unheard of, Malt beer, produced by Tuborg Turkey.

But T was due to leave in a day or two, so I thought perhaps a celebratory bottle of wine was called for. Alcohol is not exactly freely available in Turkey. There are a few bottle shops around, but very few. Most supermarkets do not sell it. However, we had discovered a branch of the French chain, Carrefour near our apartment and they had an extensive booze section. I wandered the aisles and eventually decided to support the local vintners. This turned out to be a mistake. I bought a bottle of Sava. They had some cheap stuff on the lower shelves but feeling flush I went for the top shelf, Sava Premium. It needed to breathe but after a while was, as they say, quaffable. I don't think I would buy any to lay down though.

# A Close Shave

I needed a haircut and a shave. Istanbul is full of places catering to this need at a very reasonable price. I selected a shop where the proprietor looked friendly and took a seat. I was impressed with both the haircut and the shave. Especially the shave. The barber used an old-fashioned brush to apply a foaming lather and then carefully, with a cut-throat razor, and by pinching and pulling the sagging flesh of my face, removed all traces of a beard. Once that was done, he applied a second layer of foam and repeated the process. Finally, some kind of stinging lotion was vigorously rubbed into my face. I revisited the same place a week or so later. On the second visit he concluded, without asking me, that my ears were a bit hairy. He heated some wax and applied this to my ears. After waiting a few minutes for it to solidify, he casually ripped it off. The wax took with it any recalcitrant hair, and a few layers of skin, from my ears. It was a painful process but very effective. For a couple of weeks my ears were as smooth and hair free as they have ever been.

. . .

The next day T finally made it to a *Hamam* - Turkish bath. I don't think she was too impressed. The first place we tried was in the same street as The Museum of Innocence which we also wanted to visit. Mainly because it was near where we were staying. The Museum of Innocence was created by novelist Orhan Pamuk as a companion to his novel The Museum of Innocence. The museum and the novel were created in tandem, centred on the stories of two Istanbul families. It was a strange place with some even stranger exhibits. One of the most striking was a collection of around 4000 cigarette ends, collected by the author from cigarettes smoked by the object of his obsession.

On 17 May 2014, the museum was announced as the winner of the 2014 European Museum of the Year Award.

We'd naively assumed the bath house would open fairly early but, when we passed it at 09:00am, it was closed. We went for a coffee at a nearby place which was pleasant enough but did not know much about making coffee. Just after 10:00am we returned to the bath house which now appeared open. The entrance was a bit dingy but we went in and ventured down the creaking stairway. Fortunately, I went first with T following as, when we entered, a gaggle of scantily clad young men shouted,
 - *Men only*.

. . .

Later that day, T went to the Hamam situated near to where we were staying which assured us that they had a lady's section. Her report when she returned, earlier than expected, was that this was just another marketing ploy and, as before, the main bathing area was full of hairy, overweight, leering males.

Today was T's last day in Istanbul. She'd read about a leafy suburb she wanted to visit, so we headed in that direction. On arrival in Kuzguncuk, we wandered the streets. We tried, unsuccessfully, to get an Uber to another leafy suburb nearby and had finally just taken a taxi off the street. The distance looked further on the map but turned out to be only a couple of kilometres. The taxi metre read around 35TL but we were charged 70TL. Normally I would have challenged this subterfuge but I could not summon the effort for no more than one dollar.

Kuzguncuk was pleasant enough and at least the tacky gift shops that proliferated in most other, must see, suburbs were absent. It had rained overnight and the streets were wet and glistening which made for some atmospheric photo opportunities. We walked the length of the main street passing many coffee shops before deciding to walk back to the ferry port, a distance of about two kilometres. Half way to our destination we chanced upon an exotic looking restaurant with a three- level terrace, just high enough to see over the numerous construction projects ongoing in the developing area. We entered and made our way to the top floor. The place was full of locals enjoying a Turkish breakfast. It was Saturday morning and the only item on the menu was the full Turkish. We were hungry, but not that hungry. A Turkish breakfast consists of 20 or so different dishes along with copious amounts of tea.

Later that day I walked with T to the bus stop and watched her depart for her flight to Brisbane via Seoul.

# Alone in Istanbul

It rained on and off all day today. This didn't bother me too much as I had planned a quiet day anyway. After 10 days or so of exploring the sprawling suburbs of Istanbul I was ready to stay close to home. At 10:30am the rain eased off and I walked along Istiklal Avenue, the main tourist street. It's also known historically as the Grand Avenue of Pera. Istiklal means independence and the street was thus named after Turkey's war of independence, 19 May 1919 – 24 July 1923 after which modern Turkey was formed.

From Wikipedia:
*The Turkish War of Independence was a series of military campaigns and a revolution waged by the Turkish National Movement, after parts of the Ottoman Empire were occupied and partitioned following its defeat in World War I.*

. . .

Istiklal was slightly less busy than usual, I suppose because of the rain and the fact that it was Sunday morning. During the week the street would be packed with people any time after 10:00am. Before then it would be full of haphazardly parked delivery and cleaning vehicles. I figured I should visit at least one Mosque while I was here so I was headed for the one located on Taksim square. As with all the other Mosques I'd seen, it was an imposing, architecturally interestingly designed building but when I entered there wasn't much to see. I took my shoes off in the rain and went inside. There were a few men seated in a group by the door, presumably having some kind of religious teaching bestowed on them, or maybe just talking about football, who knows?

Inside the main praying area other solitary men sat, or prostrated themselves. The walls were bare, apart from some Arabic writing on shield like objects suspended from the wall. I consulted Wikipedia to find out a little more about the building:

*Taksim Mosque is a mosque complex in Taksim Square, Istanbul. It was designed by two Turkish architects in the Art Deco style and can hold up to 3,000 worshippers. Construction began on February 17, 2017 and lasted for four years. It opened on May 28, 2021.*

I thought it looked new.

In the afternoon I wandered through a few clothes markets, vaguely looking for a T-shirt or two as I had forgotten to bring any with me. The attitude of the staff at most of the stalls was surprisingly laid back. Even when I found something I liked the look of and held it up for inspection, glancing in the direction of the stall-holder, expecting them to state a price, they didn't say anything. This was completely the opposite reaction to any restaurant or bar where, should one stop or even slow down to glance at a menu, a slightly too aggressive waiter would immediately beseech you to enter.

It always seems that, no matter how long you spend in a place, you find the best things to do and see just before you leave. I was leaving Istanbul in two days so today I found the best supermarket in the area where I had been staying. It opened at 08:00am, unusual for Istanbul, where even places one might consider for breakfast rarely opened that early. It had well laid out shelves and a friendly English-speaking check-out lady. She asked me where I was from and tried to sell me some bargain shampoo. When I laughed and pointed to my almost hairless head she said puzzlingly, in a seductive tone,
   *-Together.*

# In Search of the Lost Café

When T was in Istanbul, she had discovered, online, a café which supposedly had an Australian barista. We'd made plans once or twice to visit but they'd never come to fruition. As we'd been fairly unimpressed with our cappuccinos everywhere else, but enjoyed trying the stronger Turkish coffee, I set out today to try and find the café. On paper, or rather on Google maps, the journey looked simple enough. A train one stop north and then a 1500 metre walk. I took the train and, emerging from the station, tried to follow the Google instructions. As usual, I got a bit lost and walked up and down some steep hills for half an hour or so, before ending up back at the station. My problem was that a large hospital and a school lay between me and my destination. Following a slightly different route, which was still very hilly, I eventually found the spot where Google insisted the café should be. It wasn't there. Instead, I found a large construction site, so assumed the café had gone and would soon be replaced by more high-rise buildings.

. . .

I returned to my home ground around Istiklal and stopped off at a small place there for my caffeine fix. The coffee was delicious and the Baklava even better. I was a bit disappointed though that, despite telling the cashier that I was dining in, my Baklava came in an unnecessary plastic container and in an even more unnecessary plastic bag. And the coffee, was served in a paper cup.

I enjoy walking and I know it has health benefits. With Istanbul's snarling traffic it was often the quickest way to reach a destination. But it was a frustrating challenge as well. The cracked narrow pavements, mostly only wide enough for walking single file, did not help. But what made walking so difficult was the attitude of the locals. Changing direction just as they passed by, or stopping suddenly was rife. As was walking straight towards me, assuming I suppose that I would somehow disappear. Of course, the present-day scourge of constant phone gazing did not help.

Life in any city develops a dog-eat-dog attitude, but Istanbul was particularly bad.

# Part Four

# To Bucharest, Romania

On my last day in Istanbul, I discovered a large park just off the square. This would have been the perfect place to take my morning walk for the three weeks I'd been here. Surely preferable to struggling with the cleaning and delivery trucks blocking Istiklal Avenue. I wandered among the well laid out trees and watched a few locals play with their dogs. One, a brute of a Doberman, who would probably take an arm off if it wanted, was on this particular morning happy to chase a ball being thrown by its owner.

I took the bus to the airport. There are two Istanbul airports and consequently two buses. It's not overly clear which bus serves which. Fortunately, I'd seen T off just a couple of days before, so I knew how the system worked. I wondered if the bus company had ever considered putting up some kind of signage to help people, but it did not seem to be the Turkish way. I tried to buy a ticket:

-*Pay on the bus,* said the guy in the little booth.

-*Pay over there,* said the bus driver pointing to where I had just come from.

-*Only credit card, cash, pay the driver on the bus,* said the guy in the booth.

Payment, the odd sum of 102.50TL, around A$6, finally accomplished, I boarded and we sped through the Istanbul suburbs, as much as any vehicle could, in this traffic heavy city, to the airport of Sabiha Gokcen where my flight to Bucharest left from. This airport is on the Asian side of the city. Our route took us over the Bosphorus Bridge, known officially as the 15 July Martyrs Bridge and colloquially as the First Bridge.

I remembered that last time I had been on a bus in Turkey, 45 years previously, it was to travel from Istanbul to Erzurum, in the east of the country. I was on my way to Iran, and eventually India. An overnight journey of 12 hours. Hopefully this trip would be shorter.

We arrived at the airport an hour or so later. The scene was the usual chaos. The bus driver opened the doors to the baggage storage then disappeared. Luggage retrieval had to be done by the passengers. I was in no hurry and waited politely while everyone was done grabbing their bag.

Inside the airport I went through the various security and other checks. I was claiming a A$50 tax refund on the new phone I had bought. It struck me that the only friendly person I came across that day, was the lady who processed my claim.

My flight to Bucharest was with Pegasus airlines, a Turkish low-cost carrier. After checking in, which was a fully self-processing function, I realised I had left a small power-pack in my checked bag. I'd inadvertently done this before, on a flight out of Bangkok. There, I'd been stopped when boarding and had to go to a baggage handling desk to retrieve it, almost missing my flight. It had been a stressful experience and I did not want to do this again, so I tried and eventually succeeded, in finding a Pegasus service desk. There I waited patiently while other people did goodness knows what. I'd been waiting an hour or so when a friendly chap, who was also waiting in line, asked me what I needed. I explained and he laughed.
-*They won't care*, he said, laughing. *I once checked in with some ammunition on me.*

This inspired little confidence but just then the harassed lady who was on the desk also asked me what I wanted. When I explained she said dismissively,
-*It's OK, no problem.*

Despite their assurances I remained concerned that I'd get to the gate and have a problem there, or worse, be denied boarding. It didn't happen. The friendly fellow and the dismissive Pegasus lady were correct.

. . .

Romania impressed me from the moment I landed. The immigration officer was friendly and had a sense of humour. I'd never experienced this entering any other country. I stood in the non-EU queue and, when I proffered my Australian passport, he noticed that I had another one.
 -*What is your other passport?* He inquired.


When I showed him my British passport, he smiled in the direction of the shorter EU queue and said, with a grin,
 -*What a shame.*


I agreed. He stamped me in to his country saying,
 -*Welcome to Romania.*


There was also a sign to the same effect, in numerous languages, above the entrance to the baggage hall.


I'd been advised that the best way to reach my accommodation in central Bucharest was to take the bus. The oddly numbered 783, went direct from the airport to Piața Unirii, Bucharest's central square. This was a short walk from the apartment I had rented for five days. I followed the bus signs, expecting to find some kind of automated machine to buy a ticket. Paying on the bus was so last century. Eventually I spotted a lady, sitting in a glass booth dispensing tickets. The fare was six Romanian

Lei – about A$2.00. She wasn't happy when I gave her a 50 Lei note but, apart from a couple of one Lei notes, it was all I had. The bus rolled in and I boarded. Despite it being an airport bus there was no specific space for baggage. The only option was to place it on a spare seat. As the bus was not full, I did not feel too guilty about doing this. However, en route to town the bus made several stops and instead of people getting off, more and more got on. Just as we left the airport environs, I spotted a sign telling me that Bucharest was 16 kilometres and I guessed, wrongly as it turned out, that the journey should not take long. But I had not reckoned with Bucharest traffic. The city frequently tops lists of *most congested city in Europe and the world*. On such lists it vies with Istanbul, no surprise there, and New Delhi. People say Bangkok is congested, but it's really only so in the city centre as there are plenty of elevated freeways where traffic flows well. Here it was not the case. We chugged along, occasionally reaching more than 50 kilometres an hour, but mostly just crawling among the mass of cars, trucks and other buses heading into town. The journey took the better part of 90 minutes. Longer than the flight from Istanbul. At least I had a seat.

We finally arrived at Piața Unirii, one of Bucharest's main squares, and I alighted, more than ready for the short walk to my accommodation. But, despite the wonder of Google maps I went the wrong way. Once I realised my error, I did a 180 degree turn and was finally going where I wanted. I passed the bus stop where I had alighted some 20 minutes ago. I found my Airbnb and tried to follow the detailed instructions for entry provided by my host. Eventually I managed to open the main gate, tripping over the frame holding it in place. Fortunately, another resident arrived just after me and happily let me in to the building. He even showed me how to operate the ancient lift. This wasn't as easy as one might think, as with the old-fashioned wooden doors open, you could not see any buttons for floor selection. With the two of us and my suitcase squeezed inside, he manually closed the doors, pressed the relevant floor buttons and the lift creaked slowly upwards. On most subsequent days, unless I was carrying heavy shopping like beer or wine, or both, I took the stairs.

Once inside the apartment I familiarised myself with the light switches, pleasantly surprised that they were quite simple to use. As I inspected the various facilities, I became aware of a loud buzzing, coming from somewhere near the window. I'd activated the air conditioner when I entered and assumed it was this. Knowing I would not be able to sleep with this incessant noise, I switched off the air conditioner, assuming the noise would stop. It didn't. I switched off all the lights thinking that maybe a couple of wires were crossed and the noise was some sort of electrical problem. Still the buzzing continued. Finally, I realised the source of my displeasure was coming from my own suitcase. My electric toothbrush had activated itself and was buzzing away, ensconced in its small container.

# I Heart Bucharest

Even though it was my first day in the city I soon realised I was in love with Bucharest, apart from the traffic. This state of *polisaphilia* may have been a response to its laid-back, friendly people appealing more to my own spirit than the pushy Turks had.

I quickly learnt how to say hello and thank you. Hello - *Salut*, was easy, thank you - *mulțumesc,* was not.

I was staying in the old town so exploring was easy too. Unlike Istanbul, it was quite pleasant walking along the wide streets here without constantly having to dodge around badly parked cars, bags of rubbish and other pedestrians. In fact, the streets, for the most part, were eerily quiet, which suited me perfectly. I was later told that, during the communist era, only the party faithful had been housed in the city centre. Everyone else was accommodated in large, ugly, purpose built blocks, outside the city. This had not changed much in the intervening years and, although living conditions were now much improved, there was still little residential property in the centre of town.

Another reason I liked Bucharest was that Tuborg Green was readily available, and cost just one dollar at the supermarket. I took plenty of advantage of this during my stay.

The Museum of Bucharest was close to where I was staying and seemed as good a place as any to begin my exploration of the city. A security guard sitting on a wooden bench looked up briefly as I made my way to the entrance. I bought a ticket and meandered through the musty halls, gazing at artefacts and portraits of various members of the long gone, Romanian Royal family. The friendly ticket agent had told me, when I entered, that entrance was 10 Lei, about A$3 and that if I wanted to take photos, I'd have to pay an extra 25 Lei. I assured him I would not take photos, but I did sneak in one or two. On leaving, I wondered if I'd be stopped and charged the extra levy as there were security cameras throughout the building. But, on departure, nothing happened and, keen to practise my new Romanian language skills, I gave the ticket seller a cheery *mulţumesc* and walked nonchalantly, out of the door. The security guard outside had not moved from his seated position on the bench. The only difference in his demeanour was that he was now reading a newspaper, whereas when I arrived, he had been smoking a cigarette and gazing distractedly into the far distance.

# A Visit to Ceaușescu's Folly

On my itinerary today was a visit to the Parliament building. I'd been fascinated by this gigantic example of communist ego since reading about it, and its former resident, communist leader and renowned evil lunatic, Nicolai Ceaușescu and his even more egomaniacal wife, Elena.

I walked down wide tree-lined avenues towards the building, passing a number of other Government offices along the way. The route took me along *Bulevardi Natiunile Unite* - Boulevard of National Unity and the massive Parliament building could be seen from a way off. Its size is difficult to comprehend.

Some facts and figures from Wikipedia:
*The Palace reaches a height of 84 m (276 ft), has a floor area of 365,000 m² (3,930,000 sq ft) and a volume of*

2,550,000 m³ (90,000,000 cu ft). *The Palace of the Parliament is one of the heaviest buildings in the world, weighing about 4,098,500 tonnes (9.04 billion pounds), also being the second largest administrative building in the world. The Great Pyramid of Giza at about 5.75 million tons is about 40% heavier.*

I walked along the side of the gargantuan building, looking for an entrance, but did not find one until I turned a corner and found a helpful police officer.

 -*This entrance is for staff*, he said with a smile. *You have to enter at the front.*

This meant another long walk, back the way I had come, until I found the correct entrance, quite clearly marked as a *Visitors' Entrance* - they even had the apostrophe in the right place, which pleased me immensely. I went in and enquired about looking around inside. But this was not allowed unaccompanied. Understandable I suppose, it was a working office of The Government. Only guided tours were allowed and these were all booked out. The guy on the desk was as friendly as all other Romanians I had so far encountered. He offered to put me on a waiting list for the next tour at 11:00am, adding,

 -*But if it is full, don't be mad at me.*

I agreed not to chide him if I failed to gain entry and took a seat in the waiting area. This also served as a small art gallery and I amused myself admiring the works of art. The main reason people did not join tours they had booked, was not that they did not turn up, but more that they did not bring their passport, or, if they were Romanian, their ID card. I heard him tell a number of people that they must have their passport, nothing else was accepted. I wondered what the reason was for this. Why not allow other forms of photographic identity? I could only assume that, should a visitor attempt to commit some form of political sabotage on their tour, they could be quickly arrested and deported. It was not my lucky day. At around 10:45am I was apologetically informed that everybody had turned up. I was disappointed, but I knew I'd get over it.

Leaving the grand building, I crossed the road into a park where I took a seat in a small café. There were just a couple of other customers and it should have been a relaxing spot. But my fellow coffee drinkers were both smoking, and no matter where I sat their smoke wafted in my direction. I'm a reformed smoker. I always knew it was a dumb habit but, back in the 70s and 80s it was not quite so frowned upon, or expensive. Neither were we so aware of the health issues caused by inhaling poisonous fumes by choice. In Australia, it's hard to buy cigarettes, or any other smoking requisites. They have to be kept in unmarked, locked cupboards. The packet must be completely void of any markings as to the contents. And they cost a small fortune. So far on this trip, despite the gaudy, disgustingly graphic, depictions of pus-filled lungs, and other suppurating organs, on the packet, they had been fairly easily available. Turkey was the worst by far, where almost everyone, it seemed, was constantly puffing away. Here in Romania, it was less obvious. But, take a seat at any restaurant or bar and you could be sure some, usually young, often female, local would light up. Either a proper cigarette, with its foul obnoxious fumes or, almost as bad, but less pungent, some kind of vaping paraphernalia.

# A Stroll to the Station

I walked to Bucharest's Gara de Nord. This was the main railway station in the city, it was from where I would be taking a train to my next destination, Sinaia in a couple of days. If there's time, I like to check out departure points in a strange city. It makes the day of departure less stressful. The station was situated about two kilometres away and I thought walking, apart from the health aspect, would be interesting as I would pass through some of the city's more residential areas. Ultimately it turned out to be little more than a long walk through areas that were not particularly interesting. I did see a couple of quaint trams however. The station was small but, as it was Saturday morning, fairly busy. In addition to the standard electronic departure/arrival screens there was also an old-fashioned printed version showing all the scheduled trains. I gleaned from this that Romanian train timetables did not change much.

. . .

I took the Metro home. On arrival at my destination, I was pleasantly surprised to find, on exiting, that I had emerged at exactly the same corner where the lengthy bus journey had dropped me a few nights before. This reminded me that I should have taken the train on that first night and not sat on a crowded bus for 90 minutes. I'll know next time.


On my agenda the next day was a visit to Dimitrie Gusti National Village Museum near Herastrau Park. My Romanian friend had suggested this as a place worth visiting. Getting there meant taking a train and a tram. The multi-trip train ticket I had bought did not cover the trams, or the buses, but I was never brave enough to try using those. As is common in many countries now, you can't pay the driver and have to buy your ticket beforehand. Here in Bucharest every tram stop, and, as far as I could see, every bus stop, had a small booth situated nearby which contained a woman, it was always a woman, who dispensed the tickets. The Metro and suburban train system was a bit more up to date and had automated machines. It must be a lonely job, I thought, sat in a small box all day talking to people through a tiny sliding door. Ticket purchased I boarded the tram. To start with I went the wrong way. Changing direction, a couple of stops down the line, I was soon heading the right way. Fortunately, my destination was at the end of the line so I just stayed on board until I could go no further.

. . .

## A Stroll to the Station

The museum offered tickets for pensioners at half price. But when I bought my ticket, I failed to mention my age and the lady, in a slightly bigger booth than the bus ticket seller, ripped off a full price ticket. When I asked if the reduction was only for Romanian citizens, she seemed slightly miffed.

*-No, are you a pensioner? Retired? Why didn't you tell me?* She said, in perfect English.

I made a lame joke about looking so young and begged her to allow me to have another ticket at half price. A saving of 15 Lei, around A$5. She grudgingly acquiesced to my request and I promised not to make the same mistake again.

In the evening, I joined a free walking tour of the area near where I was staying. This allowed me to discover many places I should have visited during my short stay. One of these was the Roman Athenaeum theatre. I tried to visit the following morning before leaving the city but it was closed on Mondays. One place we spent time was *Piața Revoluției,* Revolution Square. The original name of this was *Piața Palatului,* Palace Square. It was renamed in 1989. It's the former headquarters of the Central Committee of the Romanian Communist Party. It was difficult to imagine, standing on the unassuming square, on that bright October evening, the horrors that had taken place 30 years or so previously. In late 1989 Just a few weeks before he and his wife ignominiously fled from the roof of the Palace by helicopter, Nicolae Ceaușescu had ordered his troops to open fire on protesters. Over 1000 people were killed.

# The Castle is Closed

Today was the start of my journey proper. I left Bucharest by train, bound for a town 150 kilometres away, up in the mountains. This was another of the places that had been recommended to me by an ex-colleague. He was born in Bucharest so I thought his advice would be good. For some reason the few passengers on the train had all been allocated seats in the same area. Probably to make it easier for the ticket inspector. Soon after departure I moved to a vacant seat with more space and tried to relax. A scruffy looking kid sat a few rows in front of me, playing moronic music videos on his phone, without the use of headphones. Cursing him silently, I moved again and put my own headphones on, almost drowning out the annoying racket emanating from his phone. He got off the train a couple of stops later and I saw him cross the tracks, instead of using the subway. I secretly hoped an express would come through the station and kill the little cretin. Was that wrong?

. . .

The train meandered through the foothills of the Bucegi Mountains, along a riverbank and arrived an hour or so later at my destination, Sinaia. The place I had booked for the night was only a 20-minute walk, but I took a taxi and I was glad I did as it seemed a lot further. I later realised this was because, instead of making a U-turn from the station, and heading directly to the hotel, the driver had taken me on a more scenic route through town. The fare was only 21 Lei, around A$7.00, so I did not complain too much.

I'd intended to visit Peles Castle in Sinaia, a local landmark. But the taxi driver told me it was closed. Monday again. He then offered to drive me around the area, five hours for €100. He showed me some pictures of mountains, streams and forests from a glossy brochure. I declined. I had a walk around town in the gathering gloom and retired to my room intending to take an early morning walk to the castle. The fact that it might be closed did not greatly deter me as I frequently find just seeing something from the outside is sufficient. Basking in its glory, as it were.

# Buildings of Sinaia

I had just one night here on my journey across Romania. I'd been told I had to visit Peles Castle. I hadn't been told it was closed on Monday and Tuesday. Today was Tuesday.

However, I needed the exercise so, in the early morning chill, I set out to walk the two kilometres or so, up hill after hill towards it.

There were some interesting buildings along the way; an old monastery, a restaurant in an ancient building, some local shops. This turned out to be a good thing because, as I came to within a few hundred metres of the castle, an officious fellow stepped out of his cosy wooden box and shouted something indecipherable in my direction.

. . .

It seemed I was not allowed to even approach the building when it was closed. I glimpsed a few turrets between the trees and that was it. I headed back down the hill.

Later that day I boarded a train to the next town on my itinerary, Sibiu.
　*-There will be castles there*, I said to myself. *Maybe they'll even be open.*

I arrived far too early at the station for the train to Sibiu. There was a comfortable waiting area which was well heated, but concerned I might miss the train, about 30 minutes before it was due, I wandered onto the freezing platform. Too many years in warm climates had affected my ability to endure the cold. In my youth, I would think nothing of waiting on windswept train platforms, or at breezy bus stops, assuming it was the norm. I paced up and down the platform, occasionally hopping from one foot to the other, until the train appeared. I boarded, grateful to be out of the cold. Within an hour on the train, I was manically divesting myself of layers of clothing, due to the heat.

The train journey was slow but enjoyable. It went via Brasov, a major city in the region, and many people got off there, leaving just a few of us to continue across the rolling hills in the direction of Sibiu. On arrival I ignored the waiting taxis as, from the map on my phone, it looked like another simple 20-minute walk to my accommoda-

tion. Only half of it was uphill but, as I soon discovered, the main problem was the quaint cobbled streets. These are not designed for someone lugging a wheeled suitcase. I bumped and clacked my way through the picturesque old town and found the place I had booked for two nights; Marius Homestay. Marius himself was standing in the doorway to greet me. Keen to employ my, recently acquired, Romanian language knowledge, I offered him a hearty,
 -*Salut.*

No response. He didn't seem to speak English, or German, or French, or Thai, or Danish or Hebrew, either. Apart from French and German I don't have any level of fluency in the other languages, even if they are included in my LinkedIn profile. But I can say *Hello,* and thought it might elicit a response. It didn't.

After a minute or two of linguistic stalemate, his wife appeared from a dark corner of the building and greeted me, enthusiastically waving a key. She showed me into the apartment, pointed out a few facilities and left me to explore.

The building the accommodation was situated in must have been around 300 years old. The part I was staying in was some kind of converted scullery area. The kitchen, a small room containing a fridge and microwave, had been added on and had no sink. Washing dishes had to be done in the bathroom, which wasn't overly convenient, or safe. The place reminded me of the flat T and I had rented back in the UK when we first got married, although we did have a proper kitchen, sink included.

# Sibiu, Romania

Once I had found the thermostat and adjusted the room temperature to something more conducive to sleep, I had a good night in my ancient converted scullery. I regretted this action the next morning when I awoke to a freezing cold room. Another quick adjustment and the massive radiators were soon blasting out the warmth that I required to leave my pit. In the communication we'd had before I left Australia, my Romanian friend had told me to seek out something called a *Papanași*, the local version of a donut. This wasn't hard, there were shops selling them everywhere. I purchased a sweet cheese one and took a seat in a coffee shop to enjoy it. It was a bit greasy but the sweet cheese filling was delicious. The locals seemed to love them and every other person was chewing on one version or another. Better for the health than smoking I suppose.

I continued my exploration of Sibiu. The old town consisted of a huge square with many bars and restaurants. There were also a number of churches, all built on a scale that, if God existed, would surely please him with the level of veneration their construction showed. I wandered into the Romanian Orthodox Cathedral. As is always the case in religious buildings, there were a few people scattered around inside, deep in thought, or prayer, or both. Also, I guessed, they were probably happy to be out of the cold. Certainly, that was the main reason I had entered. A priest in flowing black robes was making a few flamboyant hand gestures in front of an altar. He didn't just cross himself, but seemed to be practising for some kind of semaphore competition he was surely entering on his day off. In another part of the building a different priest was kneeling, normal for a priest you might say, but this one was ironing something on the carpet in front of the altar. The items he was pressing were small pieces of paper. I was intrigued by this, but felt it would be rude to get any closer and, in the half-light of the silent building, was unable to make out exactly what was going on.

# Follow Me, Follow You

Sitting in the sun of Sibiu's main square, I watched a number of tour groups being led around on early morning sightseeing trips. I usually avoid such things. Sure, it can be interesting to get a bit of history regarding a town or a building. Perhaps more of an insight than can be gleaned from Google. But, listening in, as the guide spouted her obviously well-worn speech, I thought it all sounded so trite. The people trailing behind her had that look of captives who would rather be somewhere else. Just one or two people at the front were engaging the leader with questions, only to show their own vast knowledge of the place they were in.

Later that day I took the train from Sibiu to Sighișoara. The train was a local, known in Romania as regional. We took in excess of two hours to cover the 89 kilometres between the two towns. The train consisted of just two carriages, or cars as they are correctly called on trains. It also made 20 stops between the two places. As I waited patiently for it to depart, a swanky looking train with *wagon lits* and *schlafwagen* emblazoned on some cars pulled in. On a white notice on the side of the gleaming train it said *Golden Eagle Danube Express Castles of Transylvania*. I checked the website and discovered this train travelled all the way from Istanbul to Budapest, on a very similar route to the one I was taking. The main difference was cost. And comfort I supposed.

My train pulled out and began to slowly make its way to the destination. Gazing out of the window at the countryside and odd farm building passing by, I felt the need for some urinary relief. I usually avoid using toilets on trains. Not so much for hygiene reasons, more out of a fear that I might get locked inside. Many trains have an electric lock of some kind and I am never sure if it's locked or not. But not this Romanian marvel. I decided to risk it. Ensuring the sturdy metal latch was in the locked position, I looked around for a light switch. I should have done this before I closed the door. There wasn't one, but fortunately a shaft of luminosity made its way through the window. At least enough for me to see what I was doing. I realised the lack of light was a plus as I lifted the seat. Hanging on to a conveniently placed metal bar with one hand, I began to relieve myself. At this moment the train hit a bump of some kind and a heavy part of the sink detached itself and crashed against my leg. I had to grin and bear it until I had finished the main task. Then I bent down and pushed the metal panel back into place, as best I could, before returning to my seat.

. . .

The journey continued. A small boy and his grandmother, I guessed it was his grandmother, maybe not, it's a hard life in the mountains, boarded. They took the seats opposite me. The tyke gazed at me longingly. He continued this unwaveringly, licking his lips. He'd spotted the bottle of water I was occasionally swigging from and seemed thirsty. I didn't really want him infecting my water with his germs but, I'm not a beast.

*-Are you thirsty?* I asked.


He didn't understand me but granny muttered something in Romanian, which I assume was a translation. He smiled and gazed even harder, not at me, but at the bottle of water I was holding. I proffered it and he happily guzzled a few mouthfuls. They both smiled at me and then he snuggled up against his grandmother and fell, sated and quenched, asleep.

# Sighișoara, Romania - Dracula's Bedroom

Arriving, almost unscathed, in Sighișoara, I once again made the mistake of deciding to walk from the station to my accommodation. *1.2 kilometres,* said Google, *mostly flat.* I set off marching imperiously passed the waiting taxis, which I knew from experience, would only cost a few dollars to cover the distance. But, I told myself, I needed the exercise and I did not have much luggage. It was all good as I strode along the street adjacent to the station and crossed a small bridge over a river. Almost there. My accommodation was in the old town. As everyone knows, apart from me it seems, most, if not all, old European towns were built in the most view worthy, or defensible, position, i.e., on the top of a hill of some kind. This was the case with Sigi, as I had already come to call it. Not only did access to my small hotel require me to scale slopes which would not have been unworthy of Everest, it also meant the streets were again constructed of cobble stones. As I had already discovered this was not the best surface to be pulling along a small, but still relatively heavy, wheeled suitcase.

## Sighișoara, Romania - Dracula's Bedroom

. . .

I finally arrived at Casa Wagner, my home for the next two days. After checking in with the less than communicative owner/reception person, I set off in search of a supermarket. This meant descending the slopes and crossing the crevasses I had been challenged by, on my initial attempt to reach my hotel. Shopping completed, I returned, now familiar with a few short cuts which saved distance, but meant scaling even steeper, man-made steps to reach the old town. I entered my room and slumped on the bed exhausted, not before illicitly borrowing some cutlery from the restaurant, now unoccupied, as I passed through it. How else would I consume the cherry yoghurt or spread the cherry jam on the bread I had bought?

Vlad Tepes, also known as Vlad the Impaler was born here in 1431. The novel by Bram Stoker is said to be inspired by Vlad's bloodthirsty ways. The name Dracul comes from his membership of The Order of the Dragon. Dracul is the Romanian word for dragon and devil.

In the late afternoon, I ventured out in search of entertainment and visited what was purportedly Dracula's bedroom. In reality this was just a building, part of which has been set up to look like the kind of place where a character like Dracula might have lived. It was an interesting, if somewhat contrived, experience and well worth the 10 Lei, A$3.00 entry fee.

. . .

The previous day, on my supermarket search, I had found that, apart from the UNESCO World Heritage old town, Sighișoara also had a very pleasant new town. Visiting it did mean descending and ascending a few hundred steps, but as the new town was the only area that had a supermarket or indeed any kind of shop, I had little choice.

At lunchtime I befriended a similarly aged fellow to myself who was also dining alone. He had attempted, unsuccessfully, to trade friendly banter with the waiter at the restaurant we had both chosen for lunch. I congratulated him on his attempt and we started chatting. He told me he came from North London, although I had guessed this by his accent, and was travelling alone for a month before going to meet his wife and son in Munich. We spoke, as travellers do, about the places we had been, both I suppose, trying to outdo the other with our tales of youthful exuberance and devil may care attitude to being on the road. I soon gave up the competition and let him regale me with his tales. He was an amiable fellow and I warmed to him, once it was established we shared a mutual dislike of cruises.

# The Cluj Malady

My new acquaintance was travelling to Cluj-Napoca, the next stop on my itinerary, on the same train as me. He had a first-class rail pass, so to be sociable I joined him in first-class, planning to pay the extra to upgrade myself. When the ticket inspector came along, he scanned my second-class ticket, saying nothing. I offered to pay the extra for being in first-class, but he just shrugged and walked away.

I arrived in Cluj feeling a little under the weather. I'd had the first signs of a cold; an itchy throat and a blocked nose, for a day or two. Now, as I got off the train, the sickness manifested itself. I stood, shivering slightly, in the cool of the late afternoon, trying to get my phone to work properly and point me in the direction I needed to walk to the small hotel I had booked. I knew it was only 300 metres away, but I did not know which way. In the end I set off in what I hoped was the right direction. Fortunately, it was. I checked in and hoping a hot shower would make me feel better, squeezed into the small en-suite shower cubicle in my room. After a minute or so getting the water flow and temperature to that magic spot, between scalding and freezing, I luxuriated under the shower's warmth. In fact, I stayed a little too long, it felt so good. Skin a lobster shade of red from the water I lay on the bed, momentarily feeling almost normal. Then my overheated body started to complain. Now I was sure I had a fever. I was burning up. Malaria or Dengue fever at least? I sincerely thought I would need to ask the friendly lady who had checked me in, to call a doctor, or have me whisked off to the hospital in a siren screaming ambulance. I lay on the bed for a good 10 minutes, trying to control my breathing and eventually, my blood, or whatever it was that the lengthy shower had caused to overheat, returned to its correct level. I'd opened the room window in an effort to cool myself. As I crawled between the sheets in the still light room, I completely forgot about this. An hour or two later I awoke, freezing cold and shivering. I closed the window and dug myself even deeper under the covers, sure that death could not be far away.

I survived the night, only to find there wasn't that much to do or see in Cluj. It had an old town which I wandered around in on a quiet Sunday morning. Apart from the huge churches, there was little of interest. One item which intrigued me were the statues, most of which depicted famous Romanians on oversized horses. Equine immensity was obviously highly prized here. I picked up some items at a Carrefour supermarket and spent the day in my room. I had one little victory, after asking a number of times, in finally being given a second pillow. I had trouble connecting to the internet and had to rely on using tethering on my phone.

I had another fitful night's sleep. The sore throat I'd been suffering from, for a day or two, meant that I woke myself up each time I tried to swallow. But what interrupted my sleep most was the frequent footfall on the stairs and in the corridors, just outside my room. The small hotel I had selected was pleasant enough, but its main attraction was its proximity to the railway station, a few hundred metres away. Romanian trains come and go at odd times of the day and night. Especially so here in Cluj, in the west of the country, close to the Hungarian border. People obviously booked rooms to prepare themselves for a trip across the border and, every couple of hours, just before a train was due to depart, I would hear some adventurous nocturnal traveller stumbling down the tiled stairs, invariably dragging a heavy suitcase, and heading for the train station.

# To Oradea, Romania

Today marked the end of my stay at the Pensiunea Junior. I finally discovered the secret knowledge required to connect to the Wi-Fi. There was a jolly looking sign in reception proclaiming, *Free Wi-Fi,* in bright blue letters and giving the password, which was simply the name of the property, with no spaces. I'd tried using this a few times, always having to double check the spelling due to my propensity to type penis instead of pensi. Not to mention the confusion caused by the plethora of vowels in the hotel name. I only ever received an error of some kind, or once or twice the always annoying and surely pointless, *connected without internet,* response. What I did not know, was which Wi-Fi to connect to. There were a few options and, naturally, I always chose the most logical one, which consisted of the hotel name, followed by some numbers. But no, the one to use was the one which bore no resemblance to anything one might have assumed, a hotel called Pensiunea Junior might use.

. . .

I walked to the station and boarded my train. Three, mostly sweltering, hours later I arrived at Oradea. I knew from past experience that Google's, *mostly flat,* opinion of any walking route was similar to the, *not far now sir,* response I had received many times while trekking in Nepal. I thought it was time to give Bolt, the local version of Uber, a go. I entered my pick up and drop off details at the station and waited patiently. Five minutes later I received a message telling me my driver had arrived. Then my phone rang,
 -*I am here*, said the driver.


After a brief discussion I realised he was at the drop off point. Somehow, I had juxtaposed the details and told the driver to pick me up at the spot I was headed for. I apologised and received a chill *cancel trip* from the exasperated driver. This had obviously happened to him before. I took a taxi from the many waiting at the station. The driver was very chatty, he gave me a running commentary of places I should visit and brief history of his home town, as we careened through the streets. It seemed a shame I only had one night here. On arrival at my accommodation, I was happy to see that the fare was cheaper than the one I had been given by Bolt. I had taken a number of taxis in Romania and was always pleasantly surprised as to how cheap they were. What I wasn't so happy about was that nobody ever seemed to wear a seatbelt. The passenger one was always strapped around the seat, making it impossible, even for a safety-aware person like myself, to use it. Each time I took a taxi, I tried to revel in the freedom of not wearing a seatbelt and ignore the inherent danger.

. . .

I was so impressed on my last day in Romania. This started even before I boarded the train with the eclectic choice of literature at the station; Dostoyevsky, Nietzsche, Plato, plus any number of local writers, were all available for the discerning traveller, and from a vending machine, no less.

I thought Paris had some fine architecture but Oradea just blew it out of the water. After checking in to my accommodation, I ventured out in search of sustenance and took so many photos I had to break my, self-imposed, five pics a day, Facebook rule and just posted everything.

-*I might just need to buy a little place here in this quaint border town*, I thought to myself, *learn Romanian and Hungarian, and let the world go away.*

Sadly, the reality was I only had one night to live out my fantasy.

# Across the Border to Hungary

The next day, I took the train from Oradea, crossing the Romanian/Hungarian border soon after departure. The border crossing was a slow process. The bureaucracy was efficient enough, but changing locomotives and shunting back and forth took forever. On the train, I chatted with a Budapest resident. He invited me for coffee in the dining car. He was travelling with his mother and, I think, was glad to get away from her and practise his English. He worked in some kind of IT support role and told me he wasn't very happy with his job.

-*But,* he said, with an air of melancholy, *it is safe.*

I felt a strong sense of empathy with my new Hungarian friend. How many times in my working life had I sat at desks, making and taking calls, wishing I were somewhere else.

# Hungarian Lungs

I only had one day in Budapest. To make the most of it, I booked myself on a free walking tour. Despite my dislike of guided tours, I'd done this previously in Bucharest, and other cities, and found it can be a good way to get a feel for a strange city. It's not free of course, as you are pretty much obliged to give the guide a tip at the end of the tour. But it's still a good way to get an overview of what a place has to offer. The tour started in a small park. I arrived in good time. The colder weather, combined with my limited bladder capacity, meant that I was soon in need of some kind of public convenience. Budapest, like many places in Europe, did not offer this facility as generously as it should have. After some searching, I eventually found a *nyilvános vécé* - public toilet, fairly close by. There was an entry fee of the equivalent of two dollars. I figured I could afford that. But, on arrival, full of anticipation at imminent relief, I found it was closed until 11:00am. Obviously, in Hungary, no-one needs to pee before then. I'm not one for public urination. Especially in a city where there are signs everywhere explaining the fine for such an act. But I decided it was worth the risk and eventually I found a quiet corner, between two hamburger stands. I felt a bit guilty, but it was hardly my fault if Budapest's local council did not provide facilities, for what is surely a basic human right.

The tour was interesting enough, but it reminded me why I seldom sign up for group activities. The guide was a bit too keen to provide a, far too detailed, history of every aspect of her beautiful city. For some reason, on this cold day, she always chose to do this in a spot shaded from the sun and therefore absolutely freezing. She had a hell of a voice on her. At one stop I made the mistake of standing too close, in the firing line as it were, and felt the full force of her hardy Hungarian lungs.

# A Meeting with an Unusual German

I had an early start the following day, continuing my journey west and crossing yet another border to Austria. The taxi drove through the wet streets of early morning Budapest. My train left from Kelenfold Station, across the river. I'd known this when I booked it, but did not realise how far it was from where I was staying. Or that it would still be dark when my train left at 08:00am. Or that it would be raining. Or that the Hungarian for train station is *vasútállomás*. At least the journey across town gave me the chance to see something of the Buda part of the city. We crossed a magnificent bridge, which links the two sides and headed towards the station. The driver, for reasons known only to herself, dropped me at a tram stop near the main station. In the half-light I sought out the route the few hundred metres to the station.

My stress level increased as I searched the departures board for my train. The only international train I could

## A Meeting with an Unusual German

see was bound for Prague. I'd experienced similar situations before and checked the number of the Prague bound train. It was indeed my train, with an ultimate destination of the Czech capital. It went via Vienna, where I had a connection to Linz. This was not uncommon in Europe and just something you had to know. Faith and confidence in one's own destination are just part of the existentialist traveller's day. A basic knowledge of European geography also comes in useful.

We rolled across the hills of Western Hungary in the misty morning light. It was good to be on a train that exceeded 100 kilometres an hour, the cruising speed of most Romanian trains. It wasn't exactly a TGV, but we did occasionally reach a speed of 150kmh. The seats were spacious, but hard, and I shifted uncomfortably for the three-hour journey.

We crossed the invisible border into Austria and arrived in Vienna. I had a connection here, to Linz, an hour to the south. I'd bought the cheapest ticket possible and knew that it couldn't be used on any other train. My connection did not leave for another 40 minutes and I spotted another train leaving in just a few minutes. On the Budapest - Vienna journey, no-one had checked my ticket at all. Throwing caution to the wind I decided to risk it, instead of waiting on the cold platform. Probably no more than a minute after I had comfortably seated myself on the warm train, a young employee of OBB, the Austrian train company, one of two as I was to discover, approached and I dutifully proffered my ticket. Her little machine buzzed with an unsatisfied buzz,

   -*Nein,* she said simply. *You have a Sparscheine (saver ticket). You are on the wrong train. Either buy another ticket or get off this train at the next stop.*

Now, I knew this was correct and I knew I was in the wrong. But, I couldn't help thinking, can you not show some sympathy? The train I had boarded was only 40 minutes earlier than the one I should have been on. It wasn't crowded and, had she possessed a shred of humanity, she might have just shrugged and told me to be careful next time. But she didn't. Her hatred of the human race was exacerbated by the fellow in the seat opposite me. By a strange coincidence, he had done the same as me and was also on the wrong train. We traded sympathetic glances. He was from Hamburg and visiting his sister who lived in Linz. I think she had bought the ticket and he didn't realise it was only valid on a particular train. I discovered all this later, as we continued our negative experience of Austrian train travel. We left the train at the next station, ready to wait for the correct one which would soon pass through the provincial town where we were temporarily marooned.

The drama should have ended here. I should have simply waited the requisite time, which was only 30 minutes, boarded the correct train and been on my way to Linz. My new buddy, a friendly chap who was probably about my age, was what I can only describe as a bit of a scallywag. A train arrived, its destination, Linz. It was not operated by OBB, one of the two Austrian train companies, it was operated by WestBahn, the other one.

-*Let's board this one anyway*, said my cheeky chum.

I wasn't sure but felt that him being German would surely mean he would do the right thing. I naively followed him and we boarded. It soon went wrong. A much more friendly ticket inspector approached, asked to see my ticket and I knew straight away that something was awry. I thought I'd use the old language excuse so I spoke to him in English, which of course he spoke, if not fluently then certainly unfalteringly enough to deal with me.

-*You either have to get off at the next stop or buy another ticket*, he said, at least in a more friendly tone than the OBB lady.

-*OK*, I said resignedly, *I'll get off.*

What I did not immediately realise was that this train, being operated by a different company, one that was in competition with OBB, did not stop at any of the stations, apart from Linz, that the OBB train did. This would have meant being stranded in an unknown Austrian town. Huge chunk of humble pie in hand, I politely approached the friendly ticket agent again, bought another ticket and stayed on the WestBahn train. It was nicer anyway. This did mean spending three times what I had paid originally. Clutching my WestBahn ticket, I explained the situation to my partner in crime and suggested he too, buy a new ticket. I put the extra expense down as a language lesson as I had had all of the conversations with the guy from Hamburg in German. We parted in Linz and, friendly as he had been, I wished I had never met him.

# In Linz, Austria

As was my habit, I walked from the station to my rented accommodation. The route was flat and there were no cobblestones. It took me through the centre of town and I looked forward to exploring further, once I'd settled in.

Later in the day I went for a walk around the old town, taking in the limited sights of Linz. It didn't possess the grandeur of Vienna or Salzburg, but I was happy enough there. It was good to have a few days in one place as, since leaving Istanbul, I had not spent more than two nights anywhere and was tired of unpacking, repacking and heading to the station. Linz lies on the Donau or Danube River and there were some river cruise patrons in town. I saw a few of them being shepherded around, looking bored. After a long walk through town, I spent the rest of the day reclining on my bed watching various shows on my tablet. Occasionally I spoke to myself in German in preparation for the conversations I would doubtless have with the locals over the next few days.

# The Surprise Astronomer

Another quiet day in Linz. An early morning cappuccino followed by a stroll through the local market. On my way home I had a pleasant surprise to discover the house where Johannes Kepler had lived for three years. Kepler was a major figure in scientific development in the late 16th and early 17th centuries. He's best known for his three laws of planetary motion. The local public university *Johannes Kepler University Linz* is named after him.

A more notorious former resident is Adolf Hitler who was born in Braunau am Inn (an Austrian town near the German border) whose family moved to Linz during his childhood. Needless to say, this fact is not openly celebrated by the locals.

I returned home, disappointed that what was surely the best bar in town, had closed up for the winter. This was an ancient train carriage that had been installed on the banks of the Donau river and obviously did a roaring trade in the summer months.

On that second day in Linz, I was pleased with my decision to avoid the more well known and glamorous cities of Vienna and Salzburg and to have chosen to spend a few days here. I also came to better appreciate the location of my accommodation. On arrival it had seemed a long way from town. But now I realised that by taking a slightly different route I was afforded an invigorating journey along by the river. Also, should I so desire, I could cross the river by a short bridge. I planned to investigate the attractions surely awaiting me there the following day. These included a lookout spot from where one could gaze on the splendour of the city.

It rained through the night and this encouraged the hardy Austrian mosquitos. After an interrupted night I discovered what I thought was some kind of electronic zapper, plugged in to one of the wall sockets. Further investigation revealed it to be an intercom system for the front door. I suppose the name, UKIE should have been a clue.

It was still gloomy the following morning. I cancelled my plan to walk across the bridge to the lookout. I needed to do a bit of shopping but it was Sunday. Most shops, and everything else, is shut on Sundays in Austria. I searched online and found a small, SPAR 24-hour store, attached to a petrol station, located about 1 kilometre away. Always happy to explore, I headed in its direction. Once there I was able to buy a couple of essential items. I had been hoping to get a spray of some kind to ward off the mosquitos but was unsuccessful. The rest of the day passed in idle contemplation, culminating in a short walk along the river bank in the late afternoon. I wasn't alone, most of the population of Linz also did this. With all the shops, and other entertainment, shut there was little else to do. I also did a bit of packing ready to leave for Stuttgart, Germany the following morning.

# To Stuttgart, Germany

Always keen to get a bit of exercise, I set-off to walk to the station. I knew it was three kilometres and that it would take about 40 minutes but it wasn't raining and I had time. I regretted my decision once or twice as I dragged my suitcase across yet another cobbled tram track as it clunked and bounced along. Eventually I made it to the station with plenty of time to spare. Linz station was a much more comfortable, and warm, place to wait for a train than anywhere in Romania or Hungary had been. There was even an official, heated waiting room, with comfortable seats and a coffee machine.

The train arrived right on time and I climbed aboard. I hadn't reserved a seat and the train was already quite full, but I found a seat and happily looked out of the window. As the train plunged through the Austrian countryside, I realised that I had seated myself next to someone who had a cold, or a hangover, possibly both. For most of the trip, he sighed deeply and tried to sleep, always by leaning on the small table in front of him. This meant it was impossible for me to leave my seat for toilet visits without disturbing him. We passed through Salzburg on time and headed for the German border. As we crossed the border, the train slowed down and crawled along at less than 50 kilometres an hour, for a while. The overhead display changed dramatically from an on-time arrival in Munich, where I was to connect to another train, of 15:31 to a later one of 15:40. This would give me four minutes to make my connection. Over the next 30 minutes or so, the train occasionally sped up, with the resulting display correcting itself a little, to an arrival of 15:34, and then slowed again. The resulting arrival time finally settling at 15:54, 10 minutes after my connecting train was due to leave. It wasn't the end of the world. There were plenty of trains from Munich to Stuttgart, my final destination. Consulting the DB website assured me that, should I miss a connection due to a late incoming train, I was allowed to take another train. This even applied on the super cheap *Sparscheine* ticket, which I had purchased. I wondered what might have happened if I'd had this experience on OBB, the inflexible Austrian carrier.

We eventually arrived in Munich. People pushed and shoved a little to make their connections but the whole situation was far more controlled than it might have been elsewhere. I found the next train to Stuttgart and boarded.

# The 20 Year Construction Project

It rained on and off all day on my first day in Stuttgart. I tried to explore the city as I was staying close to the centre and there were some fine museums and art galleries. Two things were against me; the weather and the fact that the whole of Stuttgart's city centre was one massive building site. My Airbnb host later told me this was due to the new station that was being constructed. The construction had been going on for 20 years! One of the main delays was that some trees, which grew on an adjacent park, had to be cut down and there had been many protests and delays because of this. But, 20 years? I persevered and made my way to the library. It was an interesting building but, apart from lots of books, there wasn't that much to see. I was soon ready to head home to get warm and dry. On my way I passed the main art gallery and thought I'd have a look. As is often the rule in art galleries, I had to put my bag and jacket in the cloakroom. I know they do this lest some over enthusiastic individual might knock over a priceless work of art, or even worse perhaps try to steal it. I took my wallet out of my bag but omitted to do the same with my phone. As I wandered among the works of art, I was unable to take any pictures. I contemplated returning to the *Garderobe* and retrieving my phone. But, in the end, decided it wasn't worth the effort.

In the evening, over beer, I chatted with my host. He was one of those people one meets more and more these days who had a wonderful mix of nationalities. He'd been born in Greece then moved to Canada with his family. He was now studying here in Stuttgart and living with his Russian girlfriend. He spoke fluent English, Greek and German. Plus, he told me, his Russian was OK.

I had a train to Paris to catch at 06:25am the following day so I set the alarm for 05:00am. I slept fitfully, waking up each hour and checking the time. Eventually at around 03:30am I gave up on sleep and checked my emails. I was pleased to see I'd received almost A$10 for book sales from one of my resellers. This gave me a slight thrill along with the incentive to continue my trip despite the rain.

The multilingual owner of the Airbnb had a large number of books in various languages. I leafed through a collection of letters, in the original German, written between Goethe and Schiller, while I waited. Hoping some of their genius might flow through me.

. . .

I set off to walk to the station. The route took me through a park. I'd passed this way when I arrived and thought how pleasant it would be in summer, sitting at one of the outside bars, enjoying a cold beer. At 05:30am it was a different story. Groups of men stood around smoking. Probably, they were just going to work or had finished a night shift, but it felt safest to walk smartly with my head down.

My train or, at least the platform it left from, was easy to find. I spotted a group of skinny people smoking and assumed they must also be waiting for the train to Paris.

I found a heated waiting room. Whilst it was surely better than standing on the platform with the smokers, it wasn't particularly salubrious. Most of the other occupants were sprawled across the seats or lay on the floor, sleeping. My train to Paris arrived on time and I boarded. We headed out of Stuttgart in the wrong direction, south away from France. A few minutes later, the train stopped and after five minutes or so moved off again, this time heading north, towards France. Stuttgart is a terminus and trains have to reverse for a few miles before joining other lines which head in other directions. Useful to know. No need to panic.

We moved at a reasonable pace across the flatlands of central Germany before crossing the border at Strasbourg. From there the train picked up speed and cruised at around 300 kilometres per hour, pretty much all the way to Paris.

# Lost in Montmartre

My friend M, met me in Paris. I was staying with some mutual friends who had a small flat there, close to Montmartre. Under normal circumstances it would be a 30-minute walk from the Gare de l'Est. M was a history teacher and keen to tell me all he knew about the station and the buildings nearby. Once this part of the lesson was over, we made our way on foot towards Montmartre. In the lightly falling rain, we walked at an *escargot's* pace, stopping every few minutes, as he extolled the virtues of Hausmann, who had designed much of central Paris.

I spent the day familiarising myself with the locale I was staying in. Walking around the neighbourhood that first morning, I realised I didn't know the address of my friend's place. After a while one *Rue* looks like any other. This experience reminded me of a time I had visited Tokyo on a business trip. I'd checked in to my hotel, had a shower and worked out how the lights functioned. Then, after eight hours on a plane, I figured I could do with a bit of exercise before trying to sleep. I walked out into the dusk of a Tokyo evening and strode along for 10 minutes or so, before realising that, not only did I not know the way back to my accommodation, I did not know the address, or even what it was called. I attempted to retrace my steps but kept ending up at another hotel where, if I knew anything, it was that this was not where I was staying. What could I do anyway? Go into the hotel and ask if they knew where I was staying. As the evening grew darker, along with my sense of abandonment in an unfamiliar city, I rounded a corner and there it was. My hotel. The first thing I did on entering, was grab a card with the address on it. The second thing was to make a mental note to always do this whenever I stayed anywhere unfamiliar in the future.

On returning to my friend's apartment, I made a note of the address and her phone number before venturing out again.

Later that day I went food shopping. I enjoyed refamiliarising myself with my favourite French delicacies. The lack of service at the checkouts hadn't changed.

My friend M and I spent the day exploring the city. M had been a history teacher for 50 years or more and his knowledge of the history of Paris was second to none. I tried to remember as much as I could of what he told me about the numerous buildings, monuments and statues we visited. It was a fascinating day.

We parted in the early afternoon and M made his way home. I attempted to do the same. It should have been an easy journey, but I became hopelessly confused at the Gare du Nord. I had to change from the RER-the regional train system, to the Metro. Lines were well signed but my issue was escaping from the station concourse in order to take the Metro. Every time I tried to put my ticket on the reader, it said the card was already validated. Little did I know that there was a separate exit from the station, which those with a ticket already validated had to use, to connect to the Metro. Eventually I spotted the well-hidden, secret passageway and made it out. I arrived home exhausted, happy to have a couple of quiet days, before reconvening with M on Monday for stage two of my French history course.

The next day I thought it would be prudent, in preparation for the following week, when I would return from the UK, via Paris, to travel south to Antibes, to further familiarise myself with the layout of the Gare du Nord. I was also keen to ensure I knew the way from there to the Gare de Lyon. It's a simple enough journey between the two stations. The complication is making sure you board the correct train at Gare du Nord. I completed my reconnoitre successfully but it was a challenge. It was a Saturday and extremely busy everywhere. Practice run completed, I travelled home on the Metro and was once again reminded how much I used to hate commuting. Stuffy trains, miserable people, indecipherable announcements.

Next day it rained heavily all morning. I stayed home drinking coffee and eating pastries. Later the rain cleared a little and, desperate for some fresh air, I took a walk. I was staying in Montmartre and did not need to venture far to find some picturesque areas to wander in. The recent rain made everything glisten and I took pictures of the many colourful cafés in the area, including the infamous Moulin Rouge, before the rain started up again. An early night beckoned.

# The Smallest Restaurant in the World

Today was the second day of exploring the city with M. We'd planned a literary tour but it was Monday and all the literary based museums were closed. We made our way towards what M described as the West End of Paris. This, as I was to discover, included such famous spots as the Louvre, Place Vendome and Place de la Concorde, the Champs Elysee and Arc de Triomphe.

We had lunch in a tiny restaurant. Somehow, the establishment M chose fitted 20 people into a space only big enough for maybe eight, and even then, they'd have to be good friends. The area was about the same as the bathroom in my apartment in Brisbane. We both had steak. Other options on the menu included the execrable *andouillette*, a kind of tripe sausage. When I'd first arrived in France, I'd made the mistake of ordering this in a restaurant, naively thinking it would be similar to any other type of sausage. It isn't. The establishment also served the popular and infamous *Steak Tartare*. This is nothing more than half a pound of raw mincemeat. I asked for my steak *bien cuit* - well done and I'm sure the waitress sniffed a little in disgust as I placed my order. When it arrived, I was told it had to be cut up before cooking or it would take too long.

M had his *saignant*. I had never heard of this before; it literally means bloody. I misheard and thought he had said *cendrier*, which means burnt and threw me for a minute or two until it arrived, swimming in blood and pretty much raw. As he cut into it, I watched more blood seep out onto his plate. A particular trait of the bistro was the little aprons they supplied and you could wear to protect your clothes. Presumably in case an over-enthusiastic diner sitting nearby might hack into his bleeding carcass of a steak and squirt blood across the entire eight square metres of floor space which constituted the restaurant. The size of the eating space would have served well as the banqueting hall for the king of Lilliput, but for us human sized people, it was cozy to say the least. It was a popular spot though and as we left M excitedly told me we had been sitting only a metre or so away from two well-known politicians. He also commented that they had consumed copious amounts of wine with their meal.

I would have been happy to head for home after lunch, but we continued our perambulations in the worsening rain. M's enthusiasm for, and knowledge of, the city was impressive but all I really wanted to do was get out of the cold drizzle. We stood on La Place du Concorde, with the wind howling across the vast, open plains. We took a small detour off the Champs Elysee in the direction of a famous bridge, the name of which I have forgotten. This afforded a splendid view of probably Paris's most well-known landmark, the Eiffel Tower. At least it should have done. Unfortunately, the grand structure was all but obscured by heavy, rain filled, clouds. My mood lightened as M suggested taking a bus the rest of the way down the Champs Elysee, towards the Arc de Triomphe. I was happy to do this and we boarded an almost empty bus, heading in the direction of another famous edifice. Alighting at the Arc we stood for a few minutes marvelling at its grandeur. I tried to take a picture or two but there were so many other tourists there it was virtually impossible. Finally, we walked around a corner and boarded another bus to take us back to Montmartre.

The next day marked the end of my second month away. It was also my last day in Paris, I searched the internet for somewhere close by to visit. I came across the *Musée de la Vie Romantique* - Museum of Romantic Life. It sounded like my kind of place and on arrival I was pleased to find it was free to enter.

The house the museum was situated in, built in the 1830s, was the Paris base of the Dutch-born painter Ary Scheffer. For decades, Scheffer and his daughter, hosted Friday-evening get-togethers for artistes of the day.

George Sand used to attend along with Frédéric Chopin and Franz Liszt. As I strolled through the ornately decorated rooms, I imagined a present-day equivalent where perhaps Patti Smith would be living there hosting Springsteen and Dylan.

# Safety First

I had a few minor maintenance tasks to complete at my accommodation before travelling to the UK. The friend, whose apartment it was, had asked me to ensure the gas and water were turned off before I left. I'd been shown how to do this a week or so previously when I arrived. The water was easy, a couple of simple taps, one in the kitchen and another in the bathroom. The gas was a bit more complicated. There was a button on the water heater which I found easily. I remembered I'd been told to ensure I turned this off first and then to turn off the gas supply, which was situated in a small cupboard under the sink. Accessing this was more of a challenge. The kitchen was small, but that wasn't the issue. My ancient back and even older knee made kneeling down a challenge. I bravely adopted the required position and blindly fumbled about, looking for the small lever I knew I had to turn anti-clockwise. Unable to feel my way, I grimaced, as I bent even lower, and, risking a protruding, or worse, extruding disc, finally located the lever. I repositioned it and slowly, very slowly untwisted my body and, like an ancient serpent released from its box, stood proud again.

Once these tasks were completed, I walked to the Metro for the short trip to the Gare du Nord. This turned out to be the easiest part of the day.

Despite having been there a few times previously, on arrival at Gare du Nord, I immediately got lost trying to find my way to the Eurostar check-in. Signage was minimal and after passing through a few automatic gates, which led me nowhere, I resorted to asking someone where to go. Eventually, navigating my way through the vast and ever-changing halls of the station I found my way to the check-in area. Here I stood in various queues and was duly processed. This process, like many other things, has been adversely affected by the UK's disastrous and ill-informed decision to leave the EU. I failed at the first hurdle when my ticket was rejected by the entrance bar code reader. It turned out that you could not pass the gate more than two hours before the train was due to depart. The irony here was that, before departure, numerous messages are sent telling you to arrive early.

I'd been looking forward to a proper cappuccino on the train. To my chagrin, the cappuccino machine was broken and instant coffee was all that was available. This was disappointing, as it was all I'd been drinking in the past few days. My friend's place had a variety of coffee machines but I could never summon the effort required to operate them.

It was raining when the train arrived at St Pancras, a couple of hours later. No surprise there. Trains out of St Pancras were delayed due to a signal fault. Again, no surprise. I waited a while and then boarded a train for Redhill, south of London, where my friend was meeting me. The train crawled through the grey London suburbs finally picking up speed as it headed south. Towards the end of the journey, we passed through the London suburbs of Penge and Anerley, where I was born in the middle of the last century. I wondered how much they would have changed in the intervening years. This inspired me to plan a trip there during my short stay in the UK.

D met me at Redhill station and we made our way to his house in Reigate, a neighbouring suburb. By coincidence, he lived next door to an old school friend of mine. Plans had been made for us all to get together that evening in the local pub. It was a crepuscular place, the main attraction being that the owner brewed his own beer. The rain continued to fall. The pub toilets were across a small car park meaning that, as more beer was drunk, more frequent runs were required in the increasing squally rain showers. The main topic of conversation was a storm called Ciaran. It was barrelling across the Atlantic and heading for the English Channel set to desecrate the south coast. Winds of over 100 kilometres an hour were forecast. Flights and trains were being cancelled, airports and schools were being closed. Heeding the weather warning I planned a quiet day in watching TV.

# The Still Approaching Storm

Early the next morning the promised storm had not appeared. According to the weather forecast, it was lashing the south coast and still headed my way. At 08:00am a pale sun poked through the clouds and it was a pleasant morning. I took advantage of the respite and went out for a walk, amazed that people were wearing shorts despite the weather. I had an average cup of coffee and an even more average pain aux raisins in a local café. I also changed the final one thousand Hungarian forint note that I had found in my trouser pocket. I got the grand sum of £1.83 for this. I did a bit of shopping and bought some wine for the evening before returning home. The weather soon changed and rain started falling more and more heavily as the day progressed. The rain continued for the rest of the day and I amused myself watching TV, trying in vain to find something not too inane. Around 8:00pm I gave up on this hopeless task and went to bed.

. . .

The next day Storm Ciaran had moved on and was dissipating somewhere over the North Sea. D suggested I take the train to Guildford, a nearby town. It was a pleasant trip through the Surrey countryside, across the South Downs. On arrival I walked into town over a bridge across a swollen river. My first impressions of Guildford weren't great. Directly opposite the station there was a large, uninspiring, shopping centre. On exiting the shopping centre, I found Guildford to be a very pleasant town with cobbled streets and a number of old buildings. It also boasted many coffee shops. It was cappuccino time and I passed a number of cafés, weighing up which one to honour with my custom. I eventually decided to get a coffee from a guy who was offering it from an old red telephone box. This is a new thing for me but apparently quite common now in the UK, where old telephone boxes are being repurposed. Sometimes they serve as small libraries but, most commonly, as coffee shops. The setup was ingenious. On the shelf which previously, would have housed telephone directories, sat a shiny coffee machine. Seating of course was outside. The owner had rigged up a couple of small tables with umbrellas to protect patrons from the frequent rain showers.

*-Most people just get take-aways anyway*, he told me.

I commented that he must get cold in winter.

*-I'm used to it,* he bravely responded, rubbing his hands together and shivering slightly.

I bought a pastry from another guy across the street. His setup was more salubrious, with a couple of tables displaying his wares. Then I enjoyed a delicious cappuccino served by this brave, but voluble, coffee-shop-in-a-phone-box owner. He chatted away, taking great delight in telling me, at length, why his coffee was the best in town. -*It's all about the beans,* he assured me.

# He Who is Tired of London

The next day dawned dull and rainy. The leaden skies continued to hang over southern England. D had left on an overseas trip and kindly allowed me to stay on at his place. I took the liberty of increasing the temperature on the thermostat. Even with the heat pumping out of the radiators, I still felt the need to crawl back into bed after breakfast, hoping that the rain would clear sometime. As I lay under the duvet, it occurred to me, in my rain invoked, depressed state, that I had seldom been happy in England. As a child perhaps I was, however briefly, knowing no better. Even as a teenager I just assumed it was normal to be cold for six months or so of the year. It was only when I started travelling a bit that I understood it wasn't necessary to frequently be bored, or cold and wish you were somewhere else. I think this is why, even when I visit the UK in summer, after a day or two, I feel a sense of depression descending. Now with the onset of winter, I was in a grey mood.

. . .

After an hour of luxuriating in the now warm house, feeling sorry for myself, I ventured out to explore the limited local sights. I'd been told I should visit the Reigate tunnel. It was, apparently, one of the first road tunnels ever built in England. It wasn't far away and after layering up with various items of my own, and some borrowed, clothing I felt prepared. I took a wrong turn within a spit of the tunnel, due to the new phone I'd had to buy in Istanbul failing to show me which direction to walk in. I walked through the tunnel, looked at a few posters explaining its history, then turned around and walked back home.

The next morning, my mood lightened slightly, as I packed, ready to leave D's place and go to my sister in law's, who lived a few miles away. There was a bus, but it took an hour and made 42 stops, so I decided against it and booked an Uber. I'd been asked to make sure I switched off the heating and left the house keys behind. When I booked the Uber, I was surprised when the app said it would arrive in three minutes. I panicked and quickly checked that I had everything. I left the house and waited on the street. The driver arrived almost immediately. About halfway to my destination, I realised that I had forgotten to switch off the heating. This wasn't the end of the world. D had told me he could access it remotely via the internet. I sent him a message, apologising profusely, saying he would need to do it himself. Then something clicked in my head and I checked my bag, only to realise that I had also forgotten to leave the keys behind. I had no choice but to return. I told the Uber driver what was happening and he executed a U-turn to go back to the house we had just left. At least I was able to turn off the heating when I left the keys behind. Finally, we drove off again, in the direction of Sutton, the suburb where my sister-in-law lived. The driver was a nice guy and he drove well, but sitting in the back of his Toyota, stopping and starting at never-ending traffic lights and careening around roundabouts using all three lanes, I soon began to feel slightly nauseous. I was happy when we finally arrived at my destination.

# Bring your Own Blue Plaque

Inspired by passing through the area on the train a couple of days previously, I carried out my plan to entertain myself by travelling to the part of London, where I was born and where I lived, until the age of nine. I took the train from Sutton, changing at West Norwood, to Anerley. This is where I was born in late 1954, in a small bungalow. On arrival at Anerley station, I was surprised to vaguely remember the nearby area. I was also surprised that the bungalow was only a couple of hundred metres away from the station. I recalled that, as a child, it had seemed a long way. I would often be taken there, by my mother, to catch the train, to go and visit relatives who lived in other parts of the city. I stood outside the bungalow for a few minutes and took some photographs. It seemed so much smaller than I remembered. Especially the garden, which was now overgrown, no big surprise after 60 years I suppose. However, as a kid I'd remembered there being a long path leading from the front door, through some rose bushes, which my father proudly grew, out onto the street. Now there was just a few metres of unkempt trees and grass in front of the door. As I was standing there reminiscing, a lady came out of the front door. I tried to engage her in conversation, mainly because I thought she might wonder what I was doing in front of her abode. Disappointingly, she didn't speak much English and wasn't at all interested in my story of having lived in her house when I was a kid. This was a shame because, had she been friendly, I would have asked if I could go inside and have a look around. Maybe to have stood in my old bedroom and been, just for a moment, that cute blonde child again.

Leaving the bungalow, I walked down the street a little way, remembering that my grandparents had lived at the bottom of a short hill. Again, as a child, I recalled this being quite a long walk and pretty much the boundary of my small universe. I was unable to locate where they used to live and imagine, in the intervening years, their house must have been pulled down. I remembered a park nearby where I had played as a child so I made my way in that direction. Again, it was surprisingly close and also, seemed far smaller than I remembered. I walked around the park for a few minutes, found a café to have some lunch and then it was time to leave. My journey into the past was over. I was pleased I'd made the effort to revisit the area, where I'd spent part of my childhood, and which brought back a few happy memories.

The next day was another cold but bright day. In the morning, I ventured to a small supermarket and bought some sandwiches, chocolate bars and other important items for my long train journey the following morning.

# Crossing Paris, Heading South

A day on trains. I walked to the station in the rain. Stage one of my lengthy journey was the inauspicious Thames Link service between Sutton and St Pancras. It was early morning. The train was empty enough when I boarded, but as we approached central London, it soon filled up with sad, bored looking, commuters. I thought back to the wasted hours I had spent travelling to London, only to spend more hours in pointless unfulfilling jobs. The view out of the train window was unrelentingly grey. Grey skies, grey houses with grey roofs, grey streets with, for the most part, grey or black dressed people.

We finally arrived at St Pancras and, crossing the concourse, l felt a sense of relief as I checked in for my Eurostar train to Paris.

. . .

We sped through the North Kent countryside and, an hour or so later, entered the channel tunnel. 20 minutes after that we emerged in France. It was still raining, but I felt invigorated to have escaped the foreboding fields of England. The train picked up speed and slowly the skies cleared. Just over an hour later we pulled into the Gare du Nord. I made my way in the direction of the RER, to connect with my train south to Antibes, which left from the Gare de Lyon. Even though I'd practised the route just a few days earlier I still got lost. My conclusion was that the layout of the Gare du Nord changed every few days. I asked for directions but then faced another problem. The ticket I had bought a few days previously to use on the RER was rejected.

-*It's already been used,* said the long-suffering young fellow who had assisted me with directions just a moment earlier.


He sighed a little, then waved his magic pass over the reader to let me through. As it was obvious I was an idiot, and an English one, no doubt this was easier for him than explaining that I should really buy another ticket. It wouldn't have happened in Austria. As I headed off to board the connecting train, I realised that, instead of using the valid ticket I'd purchased in advance, I'd tried to use an old ticket I'd found in my jacket pocket. One that had been there for a couple of weeks, and had, indeed, already been used.


I had a two hour wait at the Gare de Lyon and it was still cold in Paris. I went to Starbucks where I paid €5.80 for a cappuccino. This was the most I'd paid so far, even more than Austria. Starbucks was an interesting place to wait and observe other travellers. It was on a mezzanine level with a good view of the station concourse and the departure's board. I wondered where other travellers were heading on this cold damp morning. Most were well dressed and I guessed were probably business men and women, off to visit customers and sit through interminable meetings where they would discuss budgets and strategy. There were a few more casually dressed folk, mostly, if not all, much younger than me and I figured they were either visiting relatives or setting off on their own adventures. In the past I might have struck up a conversation with someone, but that sort of thing didn't happen nowadays.

Finally, the time came to board the TGV for the last leg of the day's trip. I shuffled through the gates and on to the waiting train with all the other cheapskates who had paid €19 to travel to the south of France.

On board I was pleased to find that the seat I had booked was not only facing in the right direction, I hate going backwards, but was also a single seat. As we pulled out of the station and began our journey, I sat royally admiring the Paris suburbs. The clouds cleared and, no more than 30 minutes later the sun came out. I gazed happily through the window at the bright vista beyond. The depression that had overcome me in London dissipated. We continued south as the evening descended.

. . .

A few hours later I arrived in Antibes. A place I had lived in for five years. It's a beautiful little town. The list of celebrities who have lived in Antibes is a lengthy one, including; Jules Verne, Graham Greene and F Scott Fitzgerald. Picasso is also a famous ex-resident. For some reason, the SIM I had in my phone had stopped working, but fortunately I knew where my accommodation was located and made my way there. I found the building with no trouble and also managed to enter with minimal complications. In the small apartment that I had booked, I intended to access the internet and send a message to the company from whom I had bought the SIM. I soon discovered that the internet in the apartment did not work either. This was very frustrating.

The next morning, I made my way to the SFR shop, knowing that my only option was to buy another SIM. Even this turned out to be an unnecessarily complicated process. I bought the SIM, but then for reasons I still don't understand, had to go to a *tabac* shop across the road to buy a data package. I returned to my accommodation and sent an email to the company I'd bought the original SIM from. The problem was soon sorted out, something to do with the SIM not being properly registered. This meant I now had two functioning phones. I contacted the owner of the Airbnb where I was staying and told him about the problem with the internet. He directed me to a small cupboard in the apartment, where I was to switch off and on some kind of router, modem gizmo. I did this a few times but it made no difference and I never did get the internet to work.

. . .

Later in the day I had a lunch date with an ex-work colleague. It was raining heavier than usual and we abandoned any idea of an after-lunch walk.

# Antibes, France

The following morning the rain had stopped, a keen wind had blown most of the clouds away and the sun shone brightly. What else to do but take a walk around Antibes and admire the views?

Antibes sits on a peninsula in the Mediterranean. The name derives from it being opposite the city of Nice. It was founded as a Greek colony by Phocaeans who named it Antipolis. There are some beautiful views as you walk around the peninsular, Cap d'Antibes, looking up at the Old Town to the Alps beyond. Equally spectacular views can be had, along the coastline towards Nice. On a clear day you can just about see Italy. I took some photographs and had a cup of disappointing coffee in a Danish themed coffee shop. Then I walked through the market and some backstreets and made my way back to my accommodation. One thing I noticed on my lengthy walk was the cleanliness of the streets. When I had lived in Antibes, I was constantly dodging the mess left by dogs all over the pavement. Another positive change on the streets was that, when crossing the road, cars would now actually stop for you on the crossings instead of trying to run you over. I'd like to think people had become more considerate, but I knew the reality was that this change in driving habits had come about due to a heavy police presence and fines.

Later I went out again to shop for food. The local supermarket had some self-service checkouts, just what you need when you have only a few items. Their usage and availability seemed to be based on a complex algorithm, as to when they should be open. During my stay, I visited the supermarket a few times, at different times of the day. Sometimes the self-service checkouts were open, sometimes not. Further observation revealed that management only opened them when the place was busy. No doubt a union agreement of some kind. I understand the argument against these check-outs, that they take over people's jobs. That's progress. Anyway, in France at least, if the ladies, and it usually is ladies, on the till were to make even the slightest effort to help with your purchases, maybe I would feel some sympathy for their plight. But no, they scan everything as quickly as humanly possible and hurl it towards you aggressively. Then look on passively while you try to pay for and pack everything.

One of my many fantasies was to select the least helpful lady, standing quietly while she manically scanned everything and then saying,

*-Nope, I've changed my mind,* and simply walking away.


I never did it of course, but I still dream about how satisfying it would have been. Another fantasy involves drivers who insist on tailgating when you are overtaking another vehicle and, at the same time, keeping to the speed limit. I have a couple of solutions here. One is rather hi-tech and involves focusing powerful lasers on both of the aggressor's front tyres. The other, perhaps more mechanical, but equally effective, is a fine spray of oil which would be emitted from the rear of my vehicle to obscure the speedy one's view. I think I saw a contraption similar to this in a James Bond movie. If only I had the skill to develop such things. What fun I'd have before I was arrested.

# French Service

I had another walk around town in the sunshine and took more photographs. I had forgotten what an attractive town Antibes was. During the time I'd lived there I think I appreciated its beauty. Not as much as I could have as I was working and I suppose, apart from on weekends, I never spent much time exploring the town.

At the end of my few days stay, I checked out of my accommodation and went to a nearby café where I was planning to have lunch while waiting for a friend to pick me up. I took a seat in the sun, as far away from the smoking locals as possible, and waited, and waited for some service. Eventually a miserable looking guy appeared and took away some dirty plates from an adjacent table. I caught his eye and gave him a little smile of recognition. He ignored me and went back inside. Ever hopeful, I sat a little longer, assuming that now he knew I was there he would soon reappear to take my order. My positivity proved pointless. Ten minutes later there was no sign of him, or anyone else. I left and went across the road to the train station. I knew there was a small snack bar there and I dined regally on cold quiche, which I consumed with a small bottle of red wine. I had dessert too. A granny cake, whatever that might be, and a cappuccino. It was all so delicious I had another small bottle of wine to finish. All served by a lady who, despite numerous signs, in both French and English warning; *no change for tickets*, was very friendly. It was one of the most enjoyable and satisfying meals I've ever had.

I sat in the glorious sunshine, slightly drunk, and watched the comings and goings at the station while I waited for my friend to arrive and pick me up. There were girls with huge suitcases, drunk (nothing wrong with that) looking guys still carrying cans of beer and genteel ladies and their husbands dragging shivering dogs, or carrying them in little baskets. Just another day at Antibes station.

My friends live in a lovely house in Valbonne, a village in the hills away from the coast. It's a beautiful spot but, being a few hundred metres above sea level, some degrees colder than on the coast.

We went into the village for lunch. Even though it was off season, being Sunday, the square was still packed. We managed to find a table but it was in the shade and soon became cold. After lunch we wandered through the village and it was good to see that little had changed. An evening of wine and TV shows I would not normally watch followed.

A day later I moved house again to spend a week or so with yet another friend back in Antibes. He has a proper hi-fi. This was something I had sorely missed on my travels across the world. A real hi-fi is something few people have these days. They'll either have nothing, or perhaps some kind of Bluetooth speaker. Even worse, they'll think that telling Alexa or Siri to play music is sufficient. We enjoyed a great evening listening to Van Morrison and Dylan.

# The Blue Story

I started the next day by listening to Joni Mitchell's *Blue* album, side two, of course. It reminded me of being a shy, sensitive 15-year-old, living at home and spending time, too much time, in my small bedroom at home in Herne Bay. *Blue* was one of the first albums I ever bought. Knowing that being in love with a woman, preferably a woman who looked like Joni, was all I really wanted, I'd lie on my bed gazing at the poster of her that came with the album. Not with any of the lustful thoughts one might expect from a hormonal 15-year-old. Just wanting to be in her presence. Somewhere along the way I lost the album and the poster. It was easy enough to replace the music; I own three versions of the CD and I've since repurchased the album on vinyl. Sadly, even after investing many hours searching the internet, I've yet to find the poster.

In the evening, I had dinner in Antibes with another friend. We went to an Italian place I was familiar with.

The evening was going well, until a crowd of annoying English people turned up. There were about 10 of them, but they made enough noise for 30. Exactly why they didn't realise they were not alone in the restaurant I don't know.

# Not Far Now, Sir

My host planned a walk in the hills one morning. We started with a pleasant breakfast in a *boulangerie*. After the walk we had lunch in an equally pleasant restaurant. I would have been happy to go straight from breakfast to lunch and missed out on the walk all together. The route he selected was a lung-busting, pretty much straight up, for the first 45 minutes or so, then a flat, maybe 10 minutes, with some lovely views. Finally, a knee-crackingly steep, 30-minute descent. As we walked, I was again reminded of the times I had trekked in the Himalaya in Nepal where the guide, when asked,

-*How far?* would smilingly reply,
-*Not far now sir.*


We took the train to Nice. There was a woman a few seats away who had a voice like a trombone. She would respond to her colleagues' comments and questions with a loud,

-*Oui, oui.*

When she laughed, and, unfortunately, she laughed frequently, at very unamusing things, it sounded like a machine gun.

We wandered around Nice checking out various record stores, and a hi-fi store where, after some deliberation, my friend bought a new turntable. We stopped for a coffee in *Galleries Lafayette*, a famous French department store with branches all over the country. I soon felt the need to visit the toilet. This is not so easily achieved in France. Even though we were in a large shopping centre, there was just one facility, on the top floor. I duly made my way there, knowing I would have to pay. On arrival, there was some confusion being caused by an elderly couple, standing in the entrance. They were unsure of how the system worked, and had miscalculated the amount required to carry out a basic human need. While I was attempting to help them, an even older fellow appeared and barged in front of us. Soon, he too was stymied by the complicated rules for entering the few cents required into the hi-tech machine to release the lock on the entry turnstile. Secretly, we all longed for the days when, an elderly man or woman would have been sat in a small booth and all you had to do was place a few coins in their outstretched hand.

After the toilet challenge, we left *Galleries Lafayette* and walked to the *Colline du Château* - Castle Hill. If you ever drive, cycle or walk along the *Boulevard des Anglais* you can't miss this imposing attraction. You'll see it as you leave the long straight section of the Boulevard and head around a small headland which juts out into the sea. On your left is the *Colline du Château.* It's commonly referred to as The Castle of Nice and was a military citadel. It stood overlooking the bay of Nice from the 11th century to the 18th century. It was besieged several times, especially in 1543 and in 1691, before it was taken by French troops in 1705 and finally destroyed in 1706 by command of Louis XIV. What remains is an attractive park affording stunning views in all directions along the coast.

We descended from the hill and went for lunch in Old Nice. After lunch we took the train home. It was very crowded but fortunately the trombone lady was not on board. Before departure, I needed the toilet again after consuming a few lunchtime beers and tried to use the one at the station. This also was only possible at a cost of €1. Normally contactless card payments were accepted but not today. The only option was to spend a small amount in a shop opposite and ask politely for €1 coins in the change.

# Who Wants to Live Forever?

As I travelled through Europe in late autumn and early winter, I was discovering that the warmest place in most of the houses and flats I stayed in was the kitchen. I suppose I already knew this after living in various dives in the less salubrious parts of London. Here I would sometimes sit, on colder days, with the gas rings of an ancient stove burning to provide some heat. There's always a little heat emanating from the fridge too. Also, if you stood over the toaster you could warm your hands as if you were camping somewhere and huddled over the flickering embers of a fire. Boil the kettle and, for a brief few seconds, it's a mini sauna. This last trick is harder these days with the auto cut-out most kettles have when they come to the boil. Progress foils us again.

Another Sunday came around when nothing much happened. I thought of Bowerick Wowbagger, the Infinitely Prolonged. A character from The Hitchhiker's

Guide to the Galaxy. As Douglas Adams explains in his brilliantly written book: *poor Bowerick was a being who became immortal after an accident with a few rubber bands, a liquid lunch, and a particle accelerator. After a period of total boredom, especially on Sunday afternoons, he decided to insult everyone in the entire universe in alphabetical order.*

Immortality sounds great and would probably be fun for the first few hundred, even few thousand years. What then? You'd be like the guy who returns from a trip overseas, expecting everyone to be interested in where they've been. Very soon, you realise they're not. They'd rather talk about more mundane things; football or local politics. Perhaps, a new restaurant they'd discovered.

I took a walk in the morning and had a coffee at the local boulangerie. It was OK and I managed to drink almost half of it.

I lived in the south of France for more than 10 years, but there was much of the region I had never visited. I blame this on the fact that I was usually working during the week, but it's no excuse really. I had the weekends and plenty of vacation time. I should have done more. One of the places I had not visited was Renoir's house, now a museum. It was located near the charming town of Cagnes Sur Mer. I think I tried to go there once but either got lost, or there was nowhere to park, or it was closed. This time, safely chaperoned by a friend, I made it. We arrived early and parked, the only car in the car park. We spent an interesting hour or so wandering among the artworks and olive trees. Renoir's son was a filmmaker and in one of the buildings a fascinating film he had made about the house was playing on a loop. After a look around the gift shop we headed into Cagnes itself, or more correctly, Haut de Cagnes, to visit the castle. Somewhere else I had never been. It was a steep climb to the old village, and had to be done on foot, perhaps this was the reason I had never been there. I reminded myself, it was no harder to reach than many of the places I had lugged my suitcase to in Romania a few weeks previously. We had lunch in the only restaurant open, it was a Monday so we were lucky anywhere was open at all. The restaurant owner was friendly but had a cold. We carefully cleaned the cutlery he handed us after wiping his nose. After lunch we walked across the square to the nearby castle and marvelled at the displays inside.

In the evening, I packed my bag one more time, ready for my departure to Italy the following morning. Then I spent a final hour or two enjoying music on the stereo. Probably the last time I would do so before I got home in January.

# Still on the Tracks

I had time to spare at Antibes station, but did not want to risk the undoubted disappointment ordering a coffee at the snack bar would bring. I had hot chocolate instead. I'd taken to enjoying this warming beverage, as opposed to the bitter tasting coffee so beloved by the locals. I boarded the first of four trains I was to take on my trip from Antibes to Lucca, over the border in Italy. It was still dark and a light rain was falling. I was surprised that, despite the early hour, the train was crowded and the only available seat was next to the toilet. I was hopeful it would empty out as it approached Nice. The train, not the toilet.

Many people alighted at Nice as hoped and, before more boarded, I changed seats. I did this for two reasons; it meant being further away from the toilet, and more importantly, closer to my bag. The trains that ply the French coast and cross the border to Italy are renowned for petty thievery. I had stored my bag, perhaps ill advisedly, in the luggage rack near the door, and did not want to arrive in Italy with no clean underwear. Nor the variety of pills and potions my advancing years required me to take on a daily basis.

We continued along the coast. I had no outside view from my seat, which was a shame, as I knew it was one of the best views on the Riviera, as the track winds between the cliffs and the sea. We arrived at Monaco where nearly everybody got off, and I was able to move again to a seat with more space and a view.

After another 20 minutes we reached Ventimiglia, across the border in Italy. I had my first change of trains here. The first thing I did on leaving the SNCF train was head to the station snack bar to get a cappuccino. Staff were scurrying about at the bar, but I knew how the system worked and did not make the mistake of approaching them. Instead, I went straight to the cigarette stand. I placed my order and paid and then, clutching my receipt, approached the well-dressed chap behind the counter. He glanced at the scrap of paper I had proffered and said, in a far more Italian accent than I had mustered when paying,

-*Cappuccino,* to the guy behind him, who stood poised in front of a gleaming coffee machine, which surely required a two-week training course to operate. This fellow's role in life was to prepare the beverages. I took my steaming, creamy, frothy, delicious drink to a vacant table and savoured its magnificence.

. . .

I boarded the first of many Trenitalia trains I was to take over the coming weeks. The train left Ventimiglia, picking up speed as it headed east. A few years ago, the train track, which used to follow the coast, was taken underground. The original track and stations were converted into a bike trail and refreshment stops. I'd ridden the route a few times and, for cyclists, it's a wonderful idea. However, it does make the train journey uninspiring, as it now travels through endless tunnels. After a couple of hours, mostly in the dark, we arrived in Genoa where another change of train was required. I had over an hour here to make my connection. Another cappuccino and a snack of some kind was required. No attempt at ordering in Italian was needed in the station snack bar. Large touch screens were scattered around and one simply had to poke at a few pictures to order food and drink. This was convenient, but I couldn't help thinking the days of learning, at least, a basic knowledge of the language of the country one was passing through, or visiting, would soon be over. The Star Trek universal translator could not be far away. Sadly, world peace, and a United Earth, are another matter. As are faster than light travel and the matter transporter.

From Genoa I boarded a Rome bound train. I wasn't going all the way to Rome, not yet anyway. My destination was a place called Varieggo where, once again I had to make a change for the final stage to Lucca. I accomplished this with no problem, and 20 minutes or so later, finally arrived at my destination. As always, I opted to walk to my accommodation from the station. Also as ever, I got slightly lost, but eventually arrived. The place I had selected, was suited more for those with a car, as it was a fair way out of town. Later, in search of food, I found a small *macelleria* nearby and using my limited Italian, and the owners even more limited English, managed to buy a few essential items; pasta, mortadella, mushrooms, a sauce of some kind and, most importantly, a bottle of local wine.

# Puccini Lays Down a Tune

My first full day in Lucca. I'd come here on advice from a friend back home whose wife assured me it was the most beautiful place in Italy, if not the world. From a more practical perspective, it was half-way between where I had been staying in southern France and Rome, where I was to meet T early the following month. A good place to break my journey. As I walked into town, I wondered how we would fare travelling together again. I'd been on the road alone for the better part of six weeks and, apart from a few afternoons which had dragged a bit, had enjoyed the solitude of travelling by myself. Still, I was looking forward to some company.

My plan for the day, was to visit the house where Puccini was born, which was now a museum. As I frequently do, for many things, I arrived too early. It was only 09:30am, when I pitched up at Giacomo Antonio Domenico

Michele Secondo Maria's place. While researching Puccini I noted that he'd died in Brussels.

-*Probably of boredom,* I thought to myself.


The small house did not allow visitors before 10:00am. No problem, I thought, I'll grab something at the Turandot café nearby. I was put off by the aggressively written signs, in Italian and English, on the tables outside, which read - *drinks and food purchased at the bar cannot be consumed at the tables.* I recalled being caught out by this arbitrarily applied rule of Italian life before, on the bike trip my erstwhile chum Alan and I had completed many years previously. We'd stumbled in to a small café, seeking solace from another autumnal rain shower and ordered warming beverages. When they arrived, we had dared to take a seat at one of the many vacant tables, to dry off slightly, and rest our weary legs.

-*No, no! shouted* the chief of all things coffee related. *You must pay more to sit.*


I wandered around town and didn't make it back to the museum. Everything in Lucca was very old and I was reminded of the fact that, for those from the new world, i.e., Australia and the USA, the fact that a building dated from the 15th century was a marvel. Having been raised in England and sent to school in Canterbury, where I was forced, on many occasions, to wander the sanctified stone corridors of the Cathedral, where it was invariably freezing, I was not overly impressed. Work on Canterbury Cathedral was begun in 1070.

. . .

I walked into town again the following day. My accommodation was a fair way out of the centre and I enjoyed finding different ways to the walled part, Lucca's claim to fame. Later during the few days I stayed there, I discovered there was a bus which ran once an hour. I enjoyed the walk, across the train tracks, through quiet streets and actually never saw the bus. Maybe it was pre-COVID service that had not been reinstated? I'd had a few restaurant and café suggestions from my friend in Australia, who had been to Lucca many times. I came across one café he'd mentioned almost as soon as I entered the walled town. It didn't look much and I passed by planning, once again to visit the birthplace and museum devoted to Puccini. I arrived at what I assumed was the museum. The chap behind the desk told me the museum was full. I had never heard of a museum being full, but he explained, this was due to three school groups that had just arrived.

-*Come back in 20 minutes*, he helpfully suggested.


I took the opportunity of going back to the café I had passed on my way into town to investigate its wonders. It was a small place and all the outside tables were taken. I thought this strange, as they were not in the sun, and it was late November and fairly cold even for central Italy. I went inside and ordered, happy to note there were some tables there. However, these were also occupied. I perched on a stool next to a small counter in the window. This turned out to be a good vantage point as I could not only see the passersby through the window, but also witness the locals ordering their beverages and pastries, in far more fluent Italian than I had. I stayed for the requisite 20 minutes and then made my way back to the museum. Ticket purchased, I was told the actual museum was across the road and the place I had entered was a bookshop. I headed across the road, climbed a few flights of stairs and then handed my ticket to another chap behind a desk. I wondered why he was not able to sell tickets. Maybe he was and they just wanted people to go to the bookshop first, who knows?

The small museum, like many others I had visited on this trip, consisted of a number of rooms, all full of manuscripts, clothes and other paraphernalia which once belonged to, or were used by the great man himself, or, in many cases, his friends, wives or children. My favourite item was an ancient gramophone. Verdi had used this to listen to his own music, and one would hope, that of his contemporaries.

# I Was Lying in Bed

A cold start to the day. I lay in bed waiting for the heating to warm the room. The place I was staying in had a very temperamental heating system. The stupidly tiny controller allowed me to adjust the temperature but all that seemed to happen when I did was that, set to 21 it went off and set to 22 it came on. I wasn't out to destroy the planet so I had tried turning it down to a lower temperature, or even turning it off completely overnight. The problem was, if I did that it then took two or three hours to warm the room again to a level where I did not need to sit, Scrooge-like, dressed in my entire wardrobe.

Later in the morning, as the sun warmed the cold, air I headed off to the station, to take a train the short distance to Pisa. I negotiated the complexities of the automatic ticket dispensing machine with ease, and thought I had purchased a return ticket. When, after some whirring and clunking, the little light came on in the ticket collection tray and I foraged about I could only find one ticket. I considered mentioning this issue to the lady at the *Biggli-etti* desk, and politely stood in line behind a gentleman who was negotiating some kind of complicated transaction. From behind her glass screen, the lady kindly pointed to an adjacent desk which I had not noticed. As I went towards it, the guy behind me thought he should be served first and strode to the front. I admitted defeat and concluded I would just buy another ticket, when I wanted to come back, at the station in Pisa.

I boarded the train and, as I sat studying my ticket, realised that I did, in fact, have two of them but they were stuck together. Then I started to worry as to whether Italy had a similar system to France where, even though you have bought a ticket, you still have to validate it before use at a little machine. Just another wacky rule to confuse foreigners. I had always remembered to do this in France, but wasn't sure if it was required here in Italy. I studied the back of the ticket and read that tickets must be validated. Later, when the ticket lady looked at my ticket, and scanned it with her little machine, she said nothing, so I assumed all was well.

I'd read that, instead of leaving the train at Pisa Centrale, which required a 30-minute walk to the leaning tower, one could leave at Pisa San Rosso and then it was only 10 minutes. I followed this advice and was pleased to find it was indeed correct. In fact, if you knew where to look you could actually see the tower from the station. I'd been to Pisa before but had forgotten just what an impressive site the tower is. And of course, there is much more on the site than a pendulous tower. There are 3 main buildings; the tower itself, the cathedral and the Pisa Baptistry. Despite it being late November the site was heaving with tourists. Many of them following tradition and posing amusingly as if they were pushing or holding the tower. I eschewed this childish indulgement and strolled slowly around the grounds, soaking up the atmosphere. There was a lengthy line, and a fee of €18.00, to climb the tower so I gave it a miss. As I left the site, I spotted an opportunity to take a photo of the famous edifice, between two trees. One of the trees had grown at an angle, while the other stood straight and proud. This gave the impression, depending on your angle of sight, that the tower was in fact, either straight, or leaning. This seemed a good approach to life in general and I made a mental note of it.

Leaving the tower site I walked through town, stopping for some pizza at a small stall. Pizza on a piazza in Pisa. I continued through town, crossing the Arno River and finally taking a train from Pisa Centrale back to Lucca. I liked Pisa and imagined myself finding a cosy apartment somewhere in town, spending a month there and perfecting my knowledge of Italian.

In the evening, I again picked up some items at the local *macelleria*, which I now knew meant butcher. I was developing quite a rapport, or whatever that is in Italian, with the owner. Each time I went there he seemed to know more English than on the previous visit. Also, if I tried to ask for anything in Italian, he'd politely correct me. A much better way to pick up a language than sitting in a stuffy classroom with other linguistically challenged individuals.

# Rain Falling on my Shoes

Another cold start to the day. I lay in bed again, thinking about my options; Florence, back to Pisa, or a trip to the seaside town of Viareggio. I could also have stayed in Lucca, or even just stayed in bed all day, out of the wind, which was whipping around outside. I checked the trains and decided to let fate take its course. I'd walk to the station, via a new route I had found, and then go wherever the first train to depart was headed. I felt like the guy in Luke Reinhart's wonderfully dark book - *The Dice Man*.

The new route to the station involved a short walk across a field. I'd discovered it the previous day on the way home. It shaved a good 400 metres off the trek to the station. I wasn't sure I'd use it on the day I left though. Dragging my suitcase across a grassy field might prove difficult. I'd had enough trouble with the cobbled streets in Romania.

. . .

On arrival at the station, I was torn by indecision. The next two trains both went to Pisa and while I had enjoyed my day there, I did feel I should really go to Florence. It was, after all, the birthplace of the renaissance. I bought a return ticket to Florence and wandered out to the platform. I'm not sure why. My train did not leave for another 30 minutes and, even though the ticketing hall was hardly warm, it was at least protected from the wind. As I waited, a couple of Asian looking guys arrived and looked confusedly at the arrival and departures board. I asked them where they wanted to go and then explained that *partenze,* meant departures, and *arrivi* arrivals. They seemed grateful and, when they told me they were from Vietnam, I thought it boded well for my Christmas trip to their country. How wrong this prophesy turned out to be.

The train was crowded, but not as busy as Florence itself. When we arrived, it was hard to leave the station, due to the vast number of tourists and Saturday shoppers, also heading into town. I was tempted to just get back on the next train, but steeled myself for the onslaught of walking towards the river, which was the same direction as everyone else was going. I walked by the river, jostling with the crowd, until I could see the *ponte vecchio,* one of the city's most photographed sights. I took a couple of pictures and then started to head back in the direction of the station, deciding I'd had enough fun for one day. I had planned to have lunch somewhere in town, but abandoned this idea. I walked back towards the main station, passing more Gucci and Prada type stores than I had ever seen. I was getting hungry, and thought that the ultimate irony would be a meal at McDonald's, which I had seen opposite the station when I arrived. Fortunately, this gastronomic act of savagery was averted when, on entering the station concourse, I spotted an Italian eatery. I dined on a mortadella focaccia and cappuccino.

# Heading Out for the East Coast

I dragged myself out of a warm bed again. After breakfast I also forced myself to leave a fairly warm apartment and make my way to the station. I'd pretty much exhausted the day trips from Lucca, but there was still the coastal town of Viareggio to explore. I'd changed trains there on my journey from France via Genoa, and figured it had to be worth a second look. I was wrong. As always, the train was 10 minutes late but, once it arrived, it was a non-stop 20-minute trip through the rolling Tuscan hills to Viareggio.

On arrival I left the station and made my way towards the coast along a very straight and very long street. It was Sunday and nothing much was open, except for a few small bars. I hadn't had much breakfast and was hungry, but thought I'd save myself until I reached the main attraction of the coastal strip. When I did arrive, I was again shocked by just how many people had the same idea as me, and were walking along the wide avenue beside the sea. I dodged a few cyclists and scooter riding children, before leaving the main drag and heading back into town, with the idea of finding something to eat in an out of the way place that was not full of smartly dressed locals and loud foreigners. I soon found myself back at the station and, noticing there was a train already on the platform, and that it was bound for Florence, via Lucca decided I would board. There were two reasons for this. It was warm, and there was a toilet on board. I'd tried to avail myself of the facilities at the station when I arrived but did not have the requisite 1 euro in change. I don't mind having to pay to perform an act of nature although, being British, it does gall me slightly. These days who carries change? I had exactly 92 cents in my pocket. And the facilities at Viareggio station only took cash. My plan was almost foiled when, on boarding the train I found the first carriage with a toilet was out of order. I marched through the warm carriages and soon found one that was working. Joy ensued. Relaxed, I took a seat and waited for the almost empty train to depart. A couple of minutes later a family with a small, noisy, boy boarded and along with a phone-obsessed teenage girl, took the four seats next to me. This was an odd decision on their part as the train was almost empty. I endured it for a few minutes and then moved to a quieter part of the train.

The next day dawned cold again but there wasn't any sun to brighten things up at all. I did venture out to do some shopping for my trip to Rome the next day. I wandered around town for a while and then came home to my gloomy apartment. I spent another day reclining on the bed watching videos on YouTube. I thought about working on my monthly newsletter but the day and my mood did not inspire me. In the evening, I packed my bag again ready for a not so early departure the next morning. I'd started to appreciate Lucca's charms, now that I was leaving, but was certainly ready to be going somewhere new. I was sure that Rome would be a more exciting place to spend a few days. Also, I was looking forward to being reunited with T. It had been about six weeks since we'd seen each other and said goodbye at the bus stop in Istanbul.

I'd had enough of waking up cold each morning and having to wait three hours for the ineffective heating to warm the room. The previous night I had left the heating on all night. I turned it down by a couple of degrees, but not not so much that it went off completely. I also opened the window to my bedroom. I knew this wasn't good for the environment, and I did feel a little guilty, but what to do? I slept very well and was pleased, when I woke up the next day, not to be cold.

I was ready to leave early in the morning, but my train to Florence, with a connection to Rome was not until 12:30pm. I considered taking an earlier train from Lucca, assuming they'd run once an hour. Such were the vagaries of the timetable, that there was no train at 11:30am, so my plot was foiled. I cleaned the apartment a little, rechecked my bag for the seventh or eighth time and made some sandwiches for the trip. It was only about three hours to Rome, with a break in Florence, but still, who wants to be hungry? Most stations had a coffee shop and there were vending machines on the platform but I felt it was best to be prepared.

I was looking forward to arriving in Rome. A bigger city and, I was staying somewhere close to the main station, where I assumed there would be a lot more action. I don't need much but my stay in Lucca, while it had been in a pleasant enough place, was a long way from any shops, bars or any other kind of entertainment.

I was ready to leave a good 10 minutes before 11:30am. I did not want to stand around on a cold station platform as I had done the previous few days. Having exhausted the amount of YouTube videos I could watch in one day I paced around the apartment, waiting for 11:30am to come around.

At the station, waiting for the train, the guy sitting next to me on the uncomfortable, cold metal seat hummed along happily to some music on his phone. He was using headphones and I gave him a small smile to acknowledge his thoughtfulness. The train to Florence arrived on time. This was a pleasant surprise as most of the other trains I had taken in Italy had arrived behind schedule. Normally this was no problem, apart from meaning another 10 minutes freezing on the platform. As I had a tight connection in Florence, for the train to Rome, I was happy. On boarding I scored one of the few single seats. This was good for two reasons. It gave me a safe place to store my luggage, and meant I would not get some annoying youth next to me, watching mindless videos with no headphones, on his phone.

I arrived in Florence on time and connected easily to my *Frecciarossa* - Red Arrow, train bound for Rome. This train had originated in Milan and was heading for Naples. I found my reserved seat, but sat elsewhere as the gentleman in the adjacent one was fast asleep, and I did not want to wake him. The train pulled out on time and we quickly cleared the Florence suburbs and headed into the hills of Southern Tuscany. There was a woman, an Italian relation of the trombone lady I had encountered on my way to Nice, no doubt, who talked for the entire journey. This wouldn't have been a problem, but she had a voice similar to Les Dawson or Tom Waits. It was gravelly and loud without the humour, or musical entertainment, factor. I put my headphones on, activated the noise cancelling, and listened to a podcast while I gazed out of the window at the countryside flying past. We arrived in Rome less than two hours later and I headed for the small hotel I had booked close to the station. I couldn't find it. I asked a friendly lady, touting for business at a nearby restaurant, where it might be located.

-*It's just over there,* she said brightly, pointing to a building I had already inspected.

I went back across the road to number 24 which was the address I had on my phone. I could not see the name of the hotel anywhere. I was aware from previous visits to Italy, that it is not uncommon for hotels to be located on one floor of a large older building. In desperation, I called the phone number in my reservation. Somebody with a strong Indian accent answered the phone and said he would come soon. I stood and waited in the gathering gloom, what else could I do? A few minutes later, a smiling fellow appeared and asked my name. When I told him he said,

*-Yes, you are a little late,* and showed me in to the building.

The room was small and, to be honest, a bit of a dump, with peeling wallpaper and crookedly hung curtains. But the heating seemed to work, the toilet had a seat and the shower was hot. I figured it would be OK for a couple of nights. It was conveniently located, near the main station. There were restaurants, cafés and many small shops nearby.

# A Place to Call my Own

The place I was staying in was very small, but I could live with that. It was as big, if not bigger, than some of the rooms I had called home, in shared houses in London. And I had my own shower, not a bathroom I had to share with six other guys. A bathroom I don't recall anyone ever cleaning.

I thought further, about other, usually tiny, always depressing rooms I'd lived in over the years. As a child in a London suburb, I was fortunate. I had my own bedroom in a bungalow my father had built himself. Then we moved down to the Kent coast where my parents had made the, in my opinion, rash decision to buy and run a guesthouse. During the winter months, when the place wasn't full, I was spoilt for choice. Often my room would be a large one with two or three beds and plenty of space to play. But, come the high season, when rooms could be booked by paying customers, I'd be shunted into one of the smaller rooms. Or, even worse, accommodated on a narrow bed in my parents' room. This was OK until I reached the age of 10 or 11, but after that I was not happy. A teenage boy needs privacy.


When I was around 18, I left home and went to work in the big city, London. For a while I commuted from North East Kent. A boringly repetitive 90-minute journey, each way. I did much of my reading on these mind-numbing, lengthy train journeys, needing some way of passing the time. This was long before such technological wonders as The Sony Walkman were invented. Ploughing my way through the works of Sartre and Dostoyevsky only entertained me for so long though. Usually after 30 minutes, less on warm days, I would fall asleep and dream, vivid dreams of life in pre-revolutionary Russia or pre-and-post WW2 Paris.


My meagre salary did not allow me to pay much in rent but, tired of commuting, I found a series of odd, cramped, rooms in shared houses, usually in less than attractive suburbs. I vividly remember one place where a friend already lived. There were six of them sharing a three-bedroom house in East London. They did me a favour by letting me sleep on the floor in one room. Their decision was not completely born out of kind-heartedness, as I did pay some minimal rent which meant theirs decreased a bit. One day, the house owner called round unexpectedly, when everyone was home. She was not happy about the over occupancy of her neat little house and I was asked, or rather told, to move out. My friend, out of sympathy, offered to move into another, even smaller place, with me.

## A Place to Call my Own

He spent most of his time at his girlfriend's place any way. We rented a bedsit in the trendy suburb of Regent's Park. A small room with two single beds. There was a sink in the room, luxury. A particular feature of our new abode was that, when you touched the taps with wet hands, you'd get a, fortunately mild, electric shock. I didn't stay long and moved back home again for a spell, enduring, one more time, the endless commute. I'd moved on to reading Nietzsche by then.

The main problem with my Roman holiday accommodation was that the room was also very noisy. Anyone entering or leaving nearby rooms could be easily heard, and air conditioners, when they were switched on, buzzed loudly through the thin glass of the room's small window. However, resigned to my fate, I did my best to brighten things up. I found a kettle outside in the hallway and a drinking glass so I grabbed both of those. I also came across an electric heater and made good use of it, as the heating in the room didn't seem to work as efficiently as I had first thought. I felt like a prisoner, trying to make his cell a bit more homely. Or a teenager, who covers the walls of his bedroom with posters of his favourite bands.

In the morning, I did a scouting trip to the Airbnb I'd be staying in from the weekend. I found a nice bar nearby, along with a couple of small supermarkets. It seemed like an interesting area although it was a little way out of town. I enjoyed travelling out into the suburbs on the Metro. In the afternoon I went to the Colosseum, which was close to where I was staying. It was busy, but not as busy as it had been at the Leaning Tower of Pisa. I wandered around the grounds taking pictures, as much of the other tourists, as of the fantastic buildings still standing after two millennia. In the evening, I paid too much for a bottle of wine and some snacks at a small minimarket near the hotel. Later I found a proper supermarket. Of course, I found the supermarket, which was well stocked, just after I'd paid nearly €20 for a bottle of average wine and some over salty cashews in the minimarket. The next evening, for dinner, I bought a mixed salad and some yoghurt and mineral water at the supermarket. I sat hunched over the small table in my room, eating the salad with the wooden fork provided. This was something of a challenge and, in the end, I gave up on the fork and just used my bare-hands to eat the rest of the salad. I could feel the goodness of the green leafy vegetables coursing through my veins as I shovelled it, ape-like, in to my mouth. Later I remembered the cutlery I had filched from the hotel in Romania. I hadn't fully unpacked my suitcase. There was little point as the room didn't have a wardrobe, or any other storage space.

# Italian Service

I visited the Anglo-American bookshop. It had good reviews and I thought it would be interesting. Perhaps I'd strike up a conversation with the owner and he'd offer to stock and promote my own work? I walked there past various monuments of ancient Rome. I made a mental note to visit one or two of them the following day. When I arrived at the address I had for the bookshop, I couldn't find it. Eventually, looking at the names on a building which partly matched the address I had, I noticed that it was on the first floor. It closed between 1:00pm and 2:00pm. I had arrived just before 2:00pm, so I waited the requisite 10 minutes before pressing the buzzer. A lady answered in Italian and after some hesitation let me in, telling me the shop was on the first floor. When I walked in, the lady who, I assumed, had let me in was sitting at a desk. She didn't look up or acknowledge my existence at all. Another lady came out from a back room and did at least look at me. She then returned to the back room, where I heard her speaking in Italian to somebody else. I wandered around, looking at the rather limited selection of books expecting somebody might ask if they could help me, but nobody did. It was as if they didn't really care whether I was there or not. After five minutes of idle browsing, I left. I didn't plan to rush back. I could only assume they did most of their business via the internet and mail order. Certainly, they had very little concept of customer service. My dream of conquering the Rome based ex-pat community faded and disappeared.

On the way home, I went to the recently discovered supermarket again to buy some things for dinner. I had a little victory when I spotted the option that allowed me to change the self-service till to English. I'd enjoyed trying to work out what I was doing by reading the Italian but it was certainly easier and quicker to be able to do my transactions in English.

I figured it was time to delve into the plethora of ancient sites scattered around the city. I started at the National Museum. Mainly because it was near to where I was staying. The building itself has a history. In 1981, when the original building was lying in a state of neglect, the Italian government acquired it for 19 billion lire and granted it to the National Roman Museum. Its restoration and adaptation began in 1983 and was completed in 1998. Over three floors there were a huge number of displays and exhibitions. I was soon in a state of cultural over exposure and went into the gardens to recover. Next, I strolled around the grandly named Basilica of Saint Mary of the Angels and Martyrs. Then

I headed towards the Villa Borghesi. I never found it. Just after I had passed the American Embassy which is also in the same area, I went into a subway thinking it would lead into the park, where the Villa was situated. It didn't. The subway went on and on and eventually, after passing through an underground car park, took me to the Metro station of Pigna, where I had been the previous day. I gave up on my quest, bought a Metro ticket and took the train home. Later I went back to the main Termini station to buy a ticket for the airport train. I'd be taking this the next day to meet T at the airport.

The day finally came around when I was to leave the grubby pit of a hotel room that had been my home for four long days. And three noisy nights. Leaving the keys on the dresser I took a last look around the room. I'd had no choice but to leave a few small piles of rubbish; empty pizza boxes and some wine and San Pellegrino bottles, scattered around. I didn't feel too guilty about this. No one had come to clean the room, or give me clean towels the whole time I was there. I could have died in that room and not been discovered until after the checkout time.

On the Metro to the suburb of Pigneto, where T and I would be staying, I sat between a garlic reeking local and a young fellow playing music on his phone, with no headphones, of course.

I was early to check in for my new place so I sat in a nearby café for a while, listening to the locals and understanding little.

Later that day I took the Metro back into town and the train to the airport to meet T. I was surprised at how small Rome Fiumicino airport was. The airport café didn't look much at first sight. But, as I studied the items on offer, I was impressed. Beer was expensive but half a bottle of wine could be had for the same price. A guy was making fresh pasta dishes and I ordered a delicious carbonara to go with the wine.

# Everybody Back on the Bus

The first day in Rome with T. We took an open top, hop-on hop-off tour. I'd only ever done a tour like this once before, in Hamburg, and it was disappointing. Having said to myself, that I would just go along with whatever T wanted to do, we sought out one of the many garishly coloured double decker tourist buses that congregate near Termini station. We haggled a bit with the ticket seller who, obviously keen for our business on this blustery December day, which also happened to be my birthday, immediately dropped the price from €26 to €21. We clambered aboard and, after a while, a few more passengers climbed on and the bus trundled off. I wasn't properly dressed for the occasion and was soon shivering as we passed numerous sites of ancient Rome. The trip gave us a good idea of the layout of the city and we noted one or two areas for further exploration.

. . .

We alighted near the Villa Borghesi and looked for a spot in the sun to warm up. Taking a seat at an outside table at one of the many cafés, we ordered hot chocolate. Prices were inflated, but we were in a tourist area and this was to be expected. However, when it came time to pay, an extra euro was added to the price of both beverages. Assuming a simple mistake I queried this and was told,
   *-You had a large one.*


I wanted to respond,
   *-I thought you were a waiter, not a magician.* Keeping this hilarious comment to myself, I just laughed and said,
   *-I guess there's always a new way to cheat the tourists.*


He grunted. I wrought my revenge later by leaving a 1-star review on Google.


The next day we went to the district of Trastevere. We'd both entered a writing competition the previous year, for which the first prize was a six-month sponsored stay in the BR Whiting studio. This studio was an apartment given to an organisation called *Creative Australia* by Lorri Whiting, an Australian abstract painter who was embraced by the Italian art scene. She spent many years living in Rome and exhibited in prestigious galleries across Italy, the UK and New York. She established the BR Whiting Studio as a gift to honour of her late husband, the writer B.R 'Bertie' Whiting. We didn't win the competition. We didn't find the apartment either.

     . . .

## Everybody Back on the Bus

The Rome Metro doesn't go under the Tiber river, so we took it to the closest station to Trastevere and walked from there. The area was pleasant enough but very much geared towards tourists. It was pretty quiet in December but I'd imagine it would be heaving in the summer months.

We stopped for coffee and prepared ourselves to pay €3.50 each, the standard charge in any well-known area. This contrasted with the €1.50 we paid near our accommodation. When we were ready to leave, I went to the bar to pay and was pleasantly surprised that our drinks had only cost €2.00 each. A nice change from the previous day when we had been charged €4.00 each. This positive experience brightened my mood considerably and I was happy to continue exploring Trastevere in the lightly falling rain. Despite what others may think, it doesn't take much to make me happy.

We continued our rambling on the rain soaked, glistening streets before crossing the river once again and heading in the direction of Piazza Navona where we planned to have lunch.

After lunch and the better part of a litre of *acqua frizzante,* I thought I should visit the *servizzi*. On the way I went to pay the bill and, just as I had completed the transaction, and was about to make my way to the well-hidden cubby hole that served as a toilet, a young guy decided he needed to make the call.

*-Oh well,* I thought, *he won't be long.*

10 minutes later I was still waiting. I was tempted to ask his girlfriend, who was sitting patiently, looking at her phone and seemingly unconcerned, if we needed to call a doctor. Eventually the incontinent one reappeared and joined his companion, looking none the worse for wear. I braced myself and gingerly opened the rickety door to the palace of relief. To my surprise the odour was bearable and there was no sign or residue of what the young fellow had been up to. Perhaps he'd been relieving himself in other ways? Maybe his relationship with the attractive girl, who had patiently waited for him, was not going well? It was a mystery I would never solve.

It was another wet morning and, after a trip to a fashion museum, we decided to call it a day and head for home. Walking in the rain is no fun, despite what the song says, and as the nearest Metro station was a couple of kilometres away, we thought we'd take the bus. What great views we'd get, comfortably seated, as we drove through the ancient streets of the city. The bus was full and the windows were covered in condensation. We clung on tight, standing, as the vehicle splashed through the streets, trying to catch a glimpse of the marvels outside through the misty windows. The bus deposited us at Termini where we planned to take a tram back to our accommodation. Due to an accident the trams weren't running. Once again, we piled onto a crowded Metro for our journey home.

# Crossing the Strait of Messina

We took a taxi to the station for an early departure to Taormina, Sicily. After a short disagreement about which entrance to use to enter the vast station building, we settled down to wait for our train.

When we went to board, the hi-tech QR code reader gave an error. Not a good sign. Our seats were in car two. But there was no car two. We spotted a Trenitalia employee and asked what was happening.
 -*Sit in car seven,* he said, adding, somewhat superfluously, *there is a problem.*

Nothing like stating the obvious. It wasn't clear what was going on. We did as instructed and boarded car seven, along with a number of other confused travellers. Later the guard came by, repeating,
 -*There is a problem,* he informed us we would have to

get off the train at Messina and change to another train for the final hour or so to our destination.

Announcements on the train were made in Italian and English, but it didn't help. The Italian ones were loud and clear but I caught maybe five per cent of their content. The English version was so loud as to be badly distorted and therefore equally unintelligible.

The train rolled south for six hours. We arrived at a place called San Giovanni. Here the whole train was put on a ferry to be transported across the Strait of Messina to Sicily. This was exciting and a new experience for both of us. I'm not usually keen on ferries but this one was only 20 minutes or so. I went on deck and braced myself against the keen wind blowing across the strait to admire the view.

When we docked in Sicily the confusion that had reigned in Rome became clearer. We had to change trains as the train we were on was going to Palermo in the north of the island. There was only one train on the platform in Messina and we boarded it to continue on our journey to Taormina.

# The Hills of Sicily

Getting to the apartment I had booked proved a challenge. It was only a couple of kilometres from the station and we'd arrived in daylight, so walking should have been no issue. Also, for one of the few times on the entire trip, it was flat. As we set out, we discovered there was no pavement for a good part of the way. Dragging our suitcases behind us, we made our way perilously. At least it was no problem to get our bearings. We simply had to keep the sea on our left and Mt Etna on our right. Etna's nearby presence was obvious as the pavement, when there was one, was covered in black ash. The result of a recent, relatively minor, eruption.

It was cold in the apartment and neither of us slept well. The next morning, we were awake early and ready to face the day. Taormina itself was a good two or three kilometres along the coast from where we were staying. It was also up a very steep hill. We headed to a nearby bus stop and waited for a bus which, according to the recently updated time table, ran once an hour in the off-season. The bus did not show up at the designated time. This may have been because we were far from sure what that time was. We started walking. After a kilometre or so, the bus loomed out of the early morning mist. Fortunately, we were close to a stop and hailed it successfully. It was all very convivial onboard. The driver obviously knew a number of the other passengers and chatted away as he wrestled with the steering wheel, guiding the bus up the twisty road with aplomb. Views from the bus were spectacular, with Mt Etna peeking out from behind the clouds. After 15 minutes of climbing, we were deposited at Taormina termini and walked into town. It wasn't far.

I was surprised at how big a town Taormina was. We stopped for a coffee at a café. Feeling I had had enough coffee for one day, and hoping it would warm me up, I went for a hot chocolate. Another reason for this choice was that I had looked up the Italian for hot chocolate - *cioccolata calda*, and wanted to practise my pronunciation. The irony of the word *calda* meaning hot in English amused me. The place we'd selected also had some delicious cakes on offer and we chose a couple of slices.

We walked around the *Teatro Antico*, - Greek theatre for a while. It was a spectacular place with more amazing views to Mt Etna.

We descended from the hilltop using the cable car. I've used these before with no problem. When this one set off,

I became concerned as it plummeted down the steep slope, swaying unsteadily. I knew that my mother would never have countenanced using such a device. The cable car dropped us near the coast road, but we faced a four kilometre walk back to our accommodation. Fortunately, as we were walking, a bus came along and took us halfway there. The driver was an amicable fellow and we were the only passengers. He chatted away as he expertly negotiated the winding coast road.

Today was a public holiday, the spectacularly named *Feast of the Immaculate Conception*. We feared that everything might be shut. The reality was that more restaurants, at least, were open than had been on recent days. It was a Friday and I assumed they had opened early for the long weekend. We walked to the far side of the bay where an archaeological garden was located. It was a lovely walk around the bay with views to Mt Etna and back to Taormina. On the way we stopped for breakfast at a beach café where the staff were happily singing along to the Christmas music. Normally this would have irked me, but today, due to the sunny weather, I just accepted it as some people's idea of fun.

The Italians, like much of southern Europe, take siesta time seriously. As I grow older, I'm beginning to appreciate the benefits of an early afternoon nap more and more myself. But shops closing for in excess of three hours is taking it too far. When they finally reopened at 4:00pm, we went in search of supplies. We needed a few things for dinner and to make sandwiches for another lengthy train journey the following day. At the supermarket, I used my limited Italian and asked for 100 grams of my favourite cheese. I struggle with Italian numbers, always confusing *quaranta* – 40, with *cinquanta* – 50. But 100 is easy, or so I thought, *cento*. I'd used my language skill a few times before at various shops, and never had an issue. For some reason, perhaps they had a sales drive on, the fellow behind the counter hacked a huge chunk of cheese from the slab and, before I could remonstrate, had wrapped it in numerous layers of paper and plastic, before triumphantly slapping on a price. I also tried to buy a small portion of mushrooms which I thought would complement the pasta I was planning to cook for dinner. The same thing happened,

- *Cento gram,* I said, quite clearly.

He began spooning great swathes of oil dripping fungi into a particularly large tub. Unable to guess, or even approximate, the Italian equivalent of,

-*That's enough,*

All I could do was watch helplessly, finally managing a weak,

-*Grazie,* as he handed me the results of his exuberance.

At the checkout I discovered he'd tripled my order and I'd purchased well over half a kilo of cheese and mushrooms. On a positive note, they made a delicious meal and gave me some wonderfully delirious dreams.

# Back North to Naples

We'd booked a taxi for 08:45am to take us to the station. Normally we would have walked, but rain had been forecast and we knew it was a couple of kilometres to the station. Instead of waiting in the warm apartment, T thought a better option was to lock up the apartment and go outside to stand in the rain and cold. She also had a backup plan should the taxi not turn up. As I was confident it would, the taxi did turn up. We arrived 10 minutes later at the station, ready to board our train. Before doing so we enjoyed some hot chocolate and pastries for breakfast in the station café. It was Saturday and I expected the train to be full, but it wasn't. We had a carriage pretty much to ourselves for most of the journey. As it had on the journey to Taormina, the train stopped at Messina and went on to the ferry. This time another train was also on the ferry. This was the other train from northern Sicily. The two trains were joined together once they had crossed the strait and both headed north towards Naples and Rome. The journey was a little shorter than it had been on the trip south and very enjoyable. It travelled close to the coast for most of the journey and, having seats on the left and side of the train, we had some lovely views of the water. As we approached Naples some hours later, we could clearly see Mount Vesuvius in the distance.

On arrival at Naples main station, we looked for the Metro. This resulted in a confusing few minutes as it's not a Metro as such, simply a regional train service. On arrival at our destination in the Naples suburb of Mergellina, the rain had returned and we splashed our way up a hill and along bumpy cobbled streets to the accommodation I had booked.

It was still raining the next morning but we went out anyway. We were staying close to the Bay of Naples. It was a sad sight on this wet Sunday morning. Just a few desperate joggers and cyclists were out, braving the weather. Also, some dog walkers. It was hard to decide who looked the more bedraggled; the dogs or the people walking them. We continued walking the rain drenched streets a little longer before stopping into an inviting looking *paticeria*, one of the few we found open. After a revitalising cappuccino, we agreed to head for home until the rain stopped.

An hour or so later the sun finally broke through the clouds and we set off again. This time we walked to the station to take a train a few stops to Piazza Cavour.

· · ·

Naples has one of the worst, most confusing, public transport systems I've ever come across. Nothing seemed to connect. Ticket machines frequently didn't work. There did not seem to be any kind of pass one could buy. Supposedly the various train lines, buses, metros and trams, although operated by different companies, are regulated by a single entity. An organisation called *Unico Campania*. There was little evidence of any organisation whatsoever during the few days we spent trying to get around the city.

# Day Trips to Sorrento and Pompei

The Naples transport system did its best to confuse us once again. At our local station, I bravely tried to buy tickets to Sorrento. I knew this would involve a change of train at Piazza Garibaldi, Naples main station. The machine allowed me to go through the motions of entering all the details before informing me.

*-No solution can be found.*

With an air of resignation, I bought tickets for the local train to Piazza Garibaldi, knowing we would then have to queue again, to buy more tickets for the next stage of our relatively simple journey.

At Piazza Garibaldi we waited for the train to Sorrento. The train was operated by a company with the wonderful name of *Circumvesuviano*.

. . .

The train must have been over 50 years old. It was like being on a fairground ride, as it rattled its way south via Pompei. On arrival, we left the train and walked the short distance into town. Sorrento is a lovely spot. It overlooks the Bay of Naples. Despite the plethora of Limoncello shops there are a number of interesting places to visit. In the summer season there is an elevator to take people down to the beach area but as it was off-season it wasn't operating. We decided against walking and just admired the views from the town. On a good day you can see the Isle of Capri, but today was not a good day. We enjoyed a nice lunch and headed back to the station.

That evening we entertained ourselves at the laundromat. Up until today, I'd been quite happy to wash my clothes in the shower, drying them on whatever heating appliance might be available. T insisted we do the job properly.

We spent the evening in the dingy nearby *lavanderia*, watching our dirty washing go round and round in a giant washing machine. There wasn't even a bar nearby. I was again reminded of the days of my youth. Back then, when the sheets and towels became too grungy, even for me, and when I had finally resorted to wearing the oldest, flimsiest underwear I possessed, I knew it was time to head for the laundromat. I'd trudge through the dark streets in the evening gloom clutching two large plastic bags. I'd load the contents into a slightly grubby washing machine and feed it with a few coins. Then I'd sit and wait, pompously reading a novel; probably Henry Miller or George Orwell. I was going through the *gritty reality* phase of my literary journey. Other people would make friends at the laundromat. I even had one pal who met his future wife there. Not me. My machine would finish its cycle. I'd transfer everything into a giant dryer and wait another half hour. Then I'd stumble home, usually in the rain, to make my bed and drift off to sleep in clean sheets, dreaming of happier times.

We were back on the tracks again the next day. This time bound for Pompei. Once again, we took the fairground attraction ride that passes for a passenger train and clattered out through the Naples suburbs. The archaeological site of Pompei was pretty much deserted, one of the advantages of being there in December. We had an interesting hour or so wandering among the remnants of buildings and relics. Just after 11:00am we'd seen enough and both of us were getting hungry. There was a strip of restaurants by the entrance and we chose one at random. All of them offered food and drink, very much at tourist attraction prices, i.e., about twice what we had been paying elsewhere. The various sandwiches on offer were all named after Greek deities. I had an *Apollo,* while T dined on a *Diomedes.*

Then we took the train back to Naples. I'd come to enjoy riding on the old rattling train, but would not have wanted to travel on its hard plastic seats every day, which is what I assume some of the locals were forced to do on their commute.

. . .

Back in the apartment we both commented that despite the copious amount of pastries, pizza and ice cream we'd been consuming, we still looked reasonably trim. This was until we realised that the mirror we were looking at, was at an angle which, due to the laws of physics, had the effect of making our reflection both taller and slimmer.

We discovered another rail system which had a station very close to where we were staying. All of the many Naples transport systems are short on funds and the train we boarded was, again, ancient.

We went to a café called *Gambrinus,* or to give it its full name *Gran Caffè Gambrinus.* A very classy spot with waistcoated waiters milling about. It also had possibly the highest prices in Naples, with cappuccino priced at €6.00. It was almost worth it as it was a stylish place with spectacular views across the Palazzo Reale. The prices were reasonable compared to say, *Les Deux Magot* in Paris where, if memory serves, a cappuccino, or rather the pale French version of one, would set you back the princely sum of €13.00. This did include a croissant it's true. Cappuccino *sans croissant* was a mere €9.00.

We walked home along the waterfront on our last day in Naples. We'd come to like this shambolic city with its archaic, frustrating transport system but were both looking forward to taking a modern train to Rome the following morning.

# Rome Again

We sped from Naples to Rome at 300 kilometres an hour on a *Frecciarossa* - Red Arrow train, arriving a few minutes ahead of schedule. It was good to be somewhere we were, at least vaguely, familiar with. We had lunch at a small place near the station which I had discovered when staying at the worst hotel in town.

Then we made our way to where we were spending our last couple of days in Rome. Actually, the last days of the whole European part of the trip. It was a little way out of the city and getting there involved a few stops on the Metro and then a suburban train. The Metro was crowded and we stood squashed among the locals. The train stopped frequently and more people boarded. Suddenly a woman next to me shouted in English,

-*Pay attention*, she repeated it three times. Each time louder and more aggressively than before.

. . .

## Rome Again

I was confused, thinking she was upset because my small backpack, which I was still wearing, had hit her in the face. In fact, she was warning me about a potential thief who had boarded. A ghostly looking female, who stood unblinking, right next to me. I secured my bag and zipped it under my jacket.

We arrived at our destination in Lido di Ostia. It turned out to be probably the best accommodation I had stayed in, so far, on the whole trip. It had space. Space to move, space to put things. Surfaces you could use that were not covered in useless ornaments. It was also well heated. It wasn't perfect, there was nowhere to hang towels after use. And the shower was too small. Well, there's always something.

Our last full day in Europe had arrived. We headed out to explore the early morning attractions of Lido di Ostia. But it was December and most of them were closed. There was a beach but the sand looked grey and dirty. After less than an hour we returned home and waited for it to warm up a bit.

Then we took the train, two stops back towards Rome, to the archaeological site of Ostia Antica. 2,000 years ago, this was ancient Rome's seaport, a thriving commercial centre of 60,000 people.

. . .

We'd been there before, some 20 years previously and knew it wasn't in the same league as Pompei. It was close by and we had little else to do. There was also a mediaeval village and castle in the same area, which we had not seen. The ruins were deserted and we enjoyed exploring them. A couple of hours later we made our way back to the station to find that, due to industrial action, i.e., a strike, all trains were delayed and we had over an hour to wait. It was sunny but a keen wind was blowing across the fields. We had already validated our train tickets so could do little else but try and amuse ourselves on the platform.

# Part Five

# Back to Bangkok

Our Roman Airbnb host offered to arrange a taxi to the airport for €50.00. This seemed excessive as it was only 8km away. We investigated bus options and were delighted to discover the bus would cost us €1.30 each. A much better deal. We hung around the apartment most of the day waiting for our evening flight to Bangkok. The bus to the airport took us on a tour of Lido di Ostia, which we realised was a bigger town than we had thought. We'd restricted our wanderings to the area around the station and the nearest beach. We could not help but wonder if we should not have been more adventurous. It was too late now.

At the airport, check-in processing and security were straightforward and we were soon airside with plenty of time to spare. We bought some overpriced food and wandered around for a while, as one feels obliged to do at airports. It's always been a mystery to me who actually buys anything at the airport? A pair of headphones, some local snacks maybe, but a new suit? We found a place to sit and waited to board our plane. The airport seemed very quiet. Especially as it was the last Saturday before Christmas.

On the flight, our chosen airline was assailing passengers with jolly Christmas music. This was strange for an airline based in the Middle East. And after the first five minutes or so, simply annoying. Fortunately, once we'd taken off the music stopped.

We arrived in Dubai early the next morning and sat waiting for our connection to Bangkok. It was a lengthy connection and, finding some seats at our next departure gate, we both tried to grab some sleep. I'd slept for 15 minutes at best, on the flight from Rome, and, as it was the middle of the night, I thought I'd doze off immediately. It was not to be. There were so many distractions; selfish phone users and beeping passenger trollies being just a couple. I'd almost attained a low level of slumber when a couple, who'd obviously taken advantage of the airport's shopping facilities, used the vacant seat next to me to rearrange all the purchases they had made. As they did, they carried on a lengthy, animated conversation in a language I could not understand. Satisfied that their numerous purchases were correctly arranged they wandered off. I resisted the temptation to move or hide something.

. . .

We finally arrived in Bangkok. At Suvarnabhumi International, they had a new system in place for taxis. Arriving passengers were required to take a ticket from a machine. On the ticket was a designated parking bay. You just had to walk to the parking bay and a smiling Thai taxi driver would be waiting to whisk you through the Bangkok traffic to your destination. It was a good system. It would have been even better if we hadn't scored a low number on the ticket machine. It was located adjacent to parking bay number 50. Our number was 10, so we had to walk a couple of hundred metres, in the Bangkok heat, to our cab. The driver was a nice lady and drove well. It was fairly unusual to get a female cab driver in Thailand. But less unusual than in Saudi Arabia or Afghanistan I suppose.

The next day, after a fantastic night's sleep, we headed into town to run a few errands. One of these involved another short taxi ride. Yet again the driver was female. A positive sign of the changing times.

We called into our favourite coffee shop in Bangkok. After this, a toilet visit was required. Some sort of maintenance was going on in the numerous free toilets in the shopping centre. Yes free, we weren't in Europe anymore. This gave me an opportunity to use the toilet facilities at the nearby Conrad Hotel. When I worked in Bangkok our office was right next to this luxury property. Sometimes, when I had a quiet afternoon and needed a break, I would wander into the hotel lobby through a side entrance and avail myself of the facilities as a treat.

. . .

T slept in the next morning so I went for a walk in the marvel that is Benjakiti park. I'd discovered a short cut to the park, through the grounds of the Bangkok Baptist Church, on a previous visit. I enjoyed a stroll in the cool of the morning. When I got back to the room, T was still asleep so, thoughtful fellow that I am, I went downstairs, grabbed a free, and incredibly strong, coffee and sat in the small garden of the hotel. There I listened to the birds, and the motorbikes as they passed by. A little later I took another stroll in the park, where I could hear the birds but not the motorbikes.

# An Early Morning Call

We had a flight to Da Nang in Vietnam today. Getting to the airport, checking in and security were all straightforward enough. Then we went for coffee at Starbucks and life became more complicated. I sat with the bags while T faced the interrogation process to order two cappuccinos and some apple pie; hot, cold, size, sugar, name... the questioning continued.

I layered up as we waited at the freezing departure gate. I only have a vague understanding of how air conditioning works, but I do know the temperature can be adjusted. However, in the lower levels of Bangkok's Don Muang airport, this feature has not been implemented.

Our flight to Da Nang, Vietnam was uneventful and we arrived on time. Da Nang has a very modern airport. It dates back to 1940, but was completely rebuilt in 2011.

As we queued at immigration, T wondered if her visa would be valid and I wondered if my belief that, with a British passport I didn't need one, was correct. In the end it was all very simple and the bored immigration official stamped our passports, waving us through without a word. Our next challenge was customs. We just had small bags and certainly nothing to declare. The problem was that everybody else had huge bags and parcels, but also nothing to declare. There was a queue of sorts. More of a delta which led to the single customs counter. We jostled with the other recent arrivals and, not having a trolley piled high with giant packages, were able to pass through reasonably quickly.

In the throng, waiting outside the airport, was a young chap, he looked about 15, with my name on a sign. He greeted us briefly before hurrying off, presumably in the direction of his vehicle, beckoning us to follow. We did so obediently, crossing the car park in the rain, before arriving at his car. He drove us through the misty, crowded streets of Da Nang and then along the coast, in the direction of Hoi Anh, where we were to spend a few nights.

On our first morning in Hoi Anh, we were awoken at 05:00am by the noise of a radio and the sing-song sound of Vietnamese. This went on until 06:30am when it finally stopped. We managed to drift off to sleep again for a while. This habit of early morning radio blasting out in rural areas is common in parts of Asia. It's done to wake the workers who, one must assume, cannot afford alarm clocks.

It was a rainy day. It had also been a rainy night. Our shoes, which we had left outside the previous night, were soaked. I dried them, as best I could, with the hairdryer. We waited for an hour or two hoping the weather would clear. It didn't. We put on our plastic macs, grabbed our umbrellas and headed into town. It rained all day and we returned home soaked. My shoes needed the hairdryer again. So did my socks.

We were keen to begin our exploration of Hoi Anh. First, we had to make a choice. When I'd booked the accommodation it looked, and sounded, idyllic. Surrounded by rice fields and just a short walk into town. Reviews were similarly positive, extolling the authenticity of the place and the generosity of the hosts.

It was in a lovely spot and I could hardly blame the owners for the weather. Getting into town wasn't so easy. It wasn't far, 20 minutes' walk, at most. The problem was that, on foot, the route involved crossing two small bridges. These were not sturdy, or wide enough, to accommodate vehicles as heavy as a car. As we soon discovered, Vietnam, like much of Asia, is a country dedicated to the motor scooter. These buzzing beasts were everywhere. Wobbling down streets barely wide enough to walk along and whizzing past other vehicles on gridlocked main roads. If we walked into town, the two bridges we had to cross, were used extensively by motor scooters. Crossing over them meant keeping well to the side and trying to ignore the constant beep, beep, of passing, rain-shroud covered, motor cyclists. We tried it once and vowed, never again.

There was a larger, safer road bridge but it required a lengthy detour. Too far to tackle on foot. On our next foray in to town, we were keen to avoid the dangerous bridges and tried booking a taxi through Grab. It was cheap enough. The main problem was that we were staying in a very rural area. Our accommodation must have had a street address, but I never discovered what it was. Despite this, our first attempt with Grab was surprisingly successful. The taxi arrived and took us over the wide road bridge into town.

We'd arranged to meet my sister-in law, who had flown over from London and my nephew who'd arrived from Hong Kong. The plan was to celebrate Christmas together.

Rainy day followed rainy day. Our second attempt to use Grab was less successful. We stood on the corner at the end of the small street our accommodation was on, waiting. After a few minutes, a car with the registration the app had given me, approached from the direction of town. We waved and waved but the driver ignored us and drove passed. We chased him down, splashing through the large puddles, and he eventually stopped.

## An Early Morning Call

. . .

The driver took us into town and we walked the rain-soaked streets with all the other tourists. By the end of the day, the rain had cleared a bit. We threw caution to the wind and walked back over the pedestrians and motorbikes only bridge, motorbikes tooting madly.

The rain continued. Having left all my cool weather gear in Bangkok, I was suffering in the damp weather. I'd borrowed a jumper from my nephew, Tom but now I needed some long trousers. Fortunately, the town was full of shops selling, presumably fake but still reasonable quality, North Face gear. I had bought a T-shirt the previous day. Today, I picked up a pair of rather fetching maroon hiking pants to go with it.

We entertained ourselves indoors by having a cooking class with our hosts.

I could feel a cold coming on.

# COVID for Christmas

My cold progressed through the night. I awoke the next morning with watery eyes and a runny nose. I dosed myself with Lemsip and pseudoephedrine. This highly effective decongestant is banned in many countries, including Vietnam and Thailand, because it can be converted into methamphetamine. I have no idea how, and I'm pretty sure you'd need more than the 20 tablets I had with me to make a worthwhile batch. Fortunately, it's not banned in Australia and I was glad I had had the foresight to pack it.

As the day went on, I began to feel slightly better so ventured out to meet the others. They'd hidden themselves well in a café down a little backstreet. I eventually found them.

I returned home exhausted and thought it prudent to take a COVID test. It was positive. Christmas, for me at least, was cancelled.

Christmas day dawned. T went into town to meet the others and left me to my fate. She returned a couple of hours later bearing Phad Thai, a pain aux raisins and a chocolate cookie. One of the best Christmas lunches I've ever had.

I began to feel more human in the afternoon and, as it had stopped raining, I went for a walk around the small village where we were staying. I regretted that the weather had made this difficult previously.

The next day I was feeling much better, with little more than a slight cough. I took another COVID test. This time it was negative. A Christmas miracle perhaps? We walked into town and wandered around. But this time it was different. It had stopped raining, there was a little sunshine but it wasn't too hot. It was very hard to find anything to complain about. Despite our positive last impressions of Hoi Anh and Vietnam, T and I agreed, we were looking forward to getting back to Bangkok. A place we were more familiar with. Also, we knew, that the accommodation there would be more conveniently located.

. . .

Before leaving we took a last walk around the muddy fields nearby. It was a typical Vietnamese rural scene with local people working, knee deep in mud. The taxi arrived to take us to Da Nang for our flight to Bangkok. We passed through Da Nang airport with ease and were soon in the air and on our way back to Bangkok.


It was good to be back in Bangkok where drinkable coffee was freely available. We had found a few good places in Vietnam but nowhere near the number offered in Bangkok. We'd also been subjected to a strange concoction called Salt Coffee. Assuming this could not possibly be what it sounded like; we'd tried it. Unsurprisingly it was exactly what its name implied. Coffee with salt in it. Why would you do that?

# Undiscovered Bangkok

On our first day back in Bangkok, it was good to be warm again. Also to be somewhere familiar. We wandered around some shopping centres, went to a few bars and ate some great meals. I treated myself to a pedicure and had a massage.

T suggested we make an effort to discover some new parts of town. I liked this idea as I knew that, left to my own devices, I would just wander around aimlessly, buying stuff I didn't need and eating too much. Our first voyage of discovery was to a place called The Artist's House. A supposedly hidden gem of old Bangkok. It probably was hidden a few years ago but when we visited, it had definitely been discovered and the area was swarming with Eastern Europeans. The house itself was packed out with visitors. So much so that we did not even enter. The area it was located in was interesting, and we wandered around for a bit in the heat before making our way to the MRT and heading home. One of the downsides of

Bangkok's much improved public transport system is that places which, previously could only be reached by taxi - expensive, or tuk-tuk - noisy, were now, in many cases, easily accessible from either an MRT - Metropolitan Rapid Transit, or BTS -Bangkok Mass Transit System, station.

Vietnam had been wet and cool. Bangkok was hot and hotter. Unseasonably so as, usually in December and January, the laughably named cool season, the temperature often struggled to hit 30°C. Yet, here we were nearly at the end of December and daily temperatures were peaking at 35°C. I'd forgotten just how hot Bangkok gets. The best time of day is the early morning. After 07:30am it gets hotter and hotter.

# A Day of Living Dangerously

I suggested a visit to a floating market today. Getting there wasn't simple. It couldn't be done by public transport, but required a taxi, a ferry and then another taxi. Undaunted, and eager to face the challenge, we set out. Keen to embrace technology I tried to use Grab, the local equivalent of Uber, to call a taxi. This usually saved a bit of money, but, more importantly, meant that the destination was known in advance by the driver. I had tried using Grab the day before unsuccessfully. There are so many cabs plying the streets of Bangkok that they don't usually want to go through the complication of being hailed in this way. However, this morning I had more success and after a few minutes a taxi pulled up. He took us to a Wat or Temple on the river where, we knew from previous experience, we could take a small ferry across the river. We bought our tickets for the crossing, A$1 each. Then we walked onto a rickety pier, where a small wooden boat was waiting to ferry us across the river. The driver/pilot had no shirt on. I wondered if this was due to the heat or because, should the boat capsize, he would have a greater chance of swimming to shore. The boat puttered across the river for a few minutes before safely depositing us on the opposite bank. Here, the most common thing to do was hire bikes to explore. We had done this ourselves a couple of times in the past. Once we even took our own bikes, balancing them precariously on the deck of the ferry. This time we wanted to venture further and I was off bike riding until I had had my hernia fixed. We enquired about taxis, but they were not available.

The only other option was a motorbike taxi. These are very common in Thailand, but not particularly safe. If we wanted to go to the market, we really had no choice. It was about six kilometres away. We each climbed on the pillion of two small Hondas and set off. Fortunately, the drivers of both were fairly old and drove sedately. My driver was probably my age and his bike seemed to have a slightly loose, or misaligned, front wheel. Every time we took a corner, I could feel a gentle wobble. This minor mechanical fault forced him to keep the speed down. As I sat perched precariously on the back of the seat, I was desperate to move a bit, as my hip was starting to cramp. I knew this could be fatal, so I suffered in unmoving silence.

Our drivers dropped us at what appeared to be some kind of market, although it wasn't on a river. This did not bother me much. One market is much like the other in my book. T was fixated on finding the floating part. We headed into the melee and passed a number of stalls. It wasn't too crowded and, being out of the sun, was almost enjoyable. After five minutes or so we emerged from the shelter of the market, still with no sign of anything floating. T consulted her phone. Another 800 metres apparently. It seemed we had been dropped at a different market. We walked on in the ever-increasing heat. We took a turn onto a small road which T was sure should lead to the market. Keen to confirm this, use my limited language skills and confident I could say, *which way is the floating market* in Thai, I approached a lady cooking something by the side of the road.

-*Talat nam thinai khrap,* I said.

I unconsciously waved my arms about to signify my helplessness.

She pointed down the road we had already started to take, after carefully repeating what I had already said, presumably using the correct tones so that it did not sound like,

-*Can I take you out tonight?* or something worse.

On our way down this street, we came across a delightful coffee shop and called in. The coffee was good and the many fans whirring away cooled our over-heated bodies. There were a number of old posters and newspaper cuttings on the walls, featuring a young Thai man in shorts and a singlet. In some, he was holding a trophy. This turned out to be the owner, who had been a well-known long-distance runner in his day. His son now looked after the coffee shop. The elderly gentleman was probably about my age but, no doubt, much fitter.

We continued down the street, passing a barber shop, and I made a mental note to call in on the way back. Finally, we rounded a corner and came across another market. It was still on dry land but we entered its shady portals. T had been after a new wallet and had bought one at a store in town the previous day. Today, in this market in the middle of nowhere, we came across almost identical items at less than half the price. We both bought new wallets from the jovial stall holder. Moving on, I came across something I had been after for a log time. A small water bottle and, more importantly, a strap type arrangement for carrying it around. I always felt guilty when I bought yet another plastic bottle from a store, so now I could fill this and carry it easily with me, as I explored the city in the energy sapping heat. If only I had found such a thing years before when I lived in Bangkok.

After asking a couple of people where the actual floating market might be, I finally persuaded T that perhaps it had closed during COVID. We headed back to the main road in an effort to find transportation to take us to the pier for the ferry to the mainland. A couple of young guys on small motorbikes appeared out of the heat haze and, after some price negotiation, we hopped on. The fact that my driver wasn't wearing a helmet himself, let alone offering me one, should have been a clue that he was not going to be as sedate a driver as the fellow who had brought me there. And I was right. He sped along the narrow lanes, taking corners as fast as possible, overtaking everything in sight. I'm not a nervous passenger. I used to be a driving instructor. I've taken taxis in various countries where all you can do is adopt the brace position and hope for the best. My main concern was that I knew our insurance did not cover us for motorbike accidents. I guess he'd ridden these roads for years and, despite his seemingly devil may care attitude, did not want to have an accident. Although there were times when this seemed to be his goal. My main problem was holding on as he braked hard at small intersections before accelerating away from them with equal force. Not a moment too soon we arrived, safe and sound at the ferry pier and he deposited me with a smile before shooting off in a cloud of exhaust fumes.

In the evening, we went to Govinda, a favourite restaurant from the days we lived in Bangkok. We used to meet our landlord there, Mr Tang. He was a lovely fellow. We'd been living in an apartment he owned for a few months, paying a reasonable rent, when he contacted us to say he thought the rent was too high! He reduced it by around 10%. Mr Tang lived in China, visiting Bangkok every now and then. Whenever he came into town, he would contact us and offer to take us out to dinner. He had some medical issues and would only eat very simple food himself. This did not stop him from inviting us to some of the best restaurants in town. Govinda's, located on Soi 22, was a firm favourite.

The next day we were ready for stage two of our *Discover Bangkok* experience. This involved a journey by ferry along the canal. Khlong, or canal, ferries used to constitute a major part of Bangkok's transportation system. Slowly but surely, many of the canals have been built over and turned into roads. But a few of them still exist. The main route is along Khlong Saen Saep. Two frequent services operate; one between The Golden Mount and Pratunam, the second from Pratunam to the Sriboonruang Interchange. Recently, electric ferries have begun operation from the Sriboonruang Interchange. Riding on the khlong ferry is a uniquely Thai experience. It also used to be a dangerous one, due to the haphazard boarding process. Now, following a couple of incidents, this process has been improved. No longer are you expected to clamber aboard through the wooden slats that serve as windows. Each boat has a relatively easy access point, which lines up with a raised section of the pier, from which you board. Theory has it that, should you be unfortunate enough to fall in, you will only suffer any real problems if you swallow the fetid khlong water.


Once safely boarded, we wondered why everyone was sitting on one side of the ancient wooden boat, but soon realised it was to avoid the sun. As there were no available seats in the shade, we had no choice but to endure the blazing sun as we sped down the khlong. The canals are certainly wide enough for two boats to pass, but when they do, the subsequent wake makes for a bumpy ride lasting a moment or two. An exhilarating experience but perhaps not one you'd want to last too long.

. . .

Our destination was the newly opened mall, Bang Kapi, almost the end of the line, or canal. The number of shopping malls in Bangkok is overwhelming. We didn't need to buy anything and were going there more for the ferry ride. It was pleasant enough wandering around the shiny air-conditioned building. After an hour or so we headed home. We went back to our accommodation using one of the new BTS lines, the yellow line. Some sections of this line pass over roads and buildings and are a good way above street level. There had been some mechanical issues since it opened, with wheels falling off trains. Quite dangerous when you consider the height of the track. We made it back to our part of town without incident, enjoying the views.

In our never-ending quest to discover new parts of the city, we had two more items on our agenda. We visited these over the following couple of days.

The first was Wat Pariwat. Thailand, a Buddhist country, boasts a vast number of Wats or Temples. Some are more interesting to the casual observer than others. Wat Pariwat Ratchasongkram, to use its full name, has the distinction of numerous, slightly bizarre, sculptures. These feature such characters as David Beckham, Albert Einstein, Winnie the Pooh, Captain America, and Mickey Mouse. I spotted one that was either William Shakespeare or Jesus, it was hard to tell. The eagle-eyed visitor should also be prepared to be shocked, offended even, by one or two artistic creations depicting sexual acts. This odd place reminded me of a temple I had visited with my friend Chris, who lives in Thailand. Chris and his wife run a guest house called Hidden Holiday House or HHH, near the village of Huay Phlu. It's located on the bank of the Ta Jin river in the district of Nakhon Chaisri. A beautiful spot to visit. One of the many nearby attractions is Wat Srisathong. Here's some information about the temple taken from HHH's website:

*Phra Rahu is usually depicted holding a ball in front of his mouth which symbolizes the sun and the moon. Worshippers normally come to pray here on Wednesdays and Sundays and during eclipses. It is believed that Phra Rahu can be responsible for bad luck and many people come to pray here because they have had a run of bad luck and seek to change their luck. The wife of a former prime minister came to pray here to change the government's luck at one time. As Phra Rahu is the god of darkness, when praying to him, all items used must be black. You will see black flowers, black incense, black umbrellas and trays with 8 kinds of black foods.*

*Each type of food is used to pray for different things.*

*Black grapes mean good business*
*Black liqueur means courage to risk of investments*
*Black coffee means you will get whatever you wish for*
*Black jelly means patience and careful thought*
*Black beans mean progress*
*Black sticky rice means wealth and love from family*
*Black Thai cake means rewards, success and good luck*
*Black fermented eggs mean successful contact or errands*

## A Day of Living Dangerously

. . .

The second place we wanted to visit, located in the same part of town as Wat Pariwat, was a Japanese restaurant called Hajime. There's no shortage of Japanese eating establishments in Bangkok. This one was different. Once your order had been placed, you'd be served by a robot. We had an address and a friend of ours, who had visited previously, told us it was in a shopping centre. We found the address but could see no shopping centre. We stumbled around unsuccessfully in the heat, searching for the restaurant. As we did so, we passed a street vendor whose dog took a dislike to T and, snarling ferociously, nipped her on the back of the leg. Fortunately he didn't draw blood but it gave her a fright. After a while we asked directions from a local shopkeeper who sent us back the way we had come. This meant passing by the evil dog again and T took the precaution of brandishing a large tree branch as we approached the vendor's cart. The vendor saw us coming and held on to his dog. This time the animal seemed less interested and ignored us. The large stick may have helped.

Hajime's turned out to be in a small, otherwise largely unoccupied, building. We arrived before the restaurant opened but were pleased to see a small place called *Croissanterie* on the same floor. It was fast approaching coffee time so in we went.

-*Two cappuccinos please*, I said.
-*Only croissant*, replied the owner.

. . .

This made no sense. We were in a relatively unpopulated part of town. What could be the business case for a shop which only sold croissants? Surely it had to be a money laundering scheme of some kind. There was little else to do around the area. We had two hours to kill before the Japanese restaurant opened and we agreed we weren't that desperate to experience the robot café after all.

We went to Icon Siam, another of the many, too many, shopping centres which proliferate in Bangkok. In search of sustenance we took escalator after escalator to the top floor. There we found a French themed place called, unsurprisingly, *Boulangerie*. The view was spectacular, the coffee average and the music awful. To add more to my displeasure at our dining choice, and silent vow never to return, they used the crafty pricing system where neither VAT at 7%, nor service at 10%, are shown on the menu. While prices seem reasonable when you order, when it comes time to pay, they aren't.

In search of familiarity, we set off for MBK, or the Mahbunkhrong Centre. This eight-storey shopping centre has been open since 1985 and is something of an institution in Bangkok. Easy to reach, being at the end of one of the older BTS lines, it was somewhere we were more than familiar with. We were in search of a pizza place we used to frequent. We searched for a while then admitted defeat, it had gone, taken over by Sizzler. We had lunch at an establishment called Coco Ichibanya, a Japanese curry place. The menu, various types of curry-based options, allowed you to choose your *spicy level*. 1

chilli denoted mild, while 24 was described as crazy hot. Distorted pop music played through the speakers above our heads. Four girls in their early twenties who had, judging by their accents, been schooled in the USA talked vacuously at an adjacent table. I tried not to let it get to me, but their whining, pointless conversation about the fascinating subject of waking up time, soon drove me to the edge of despair and back. Each phrase was, begun by, or liberally interspersed, with a superfluous, *like*.

Back in the apartment, the air conditioner started to drip. I informed reception and a few minutes later a team of three came to investigate. One was a cleaner who mopped up the water and judiciously placed a plastic bowl to catch any further drips. The second was some kind of engineer who carried a small pipe, the purpose of which I never discovered. He removed the air filters and gave them a clean, then announced, via the third person, some kind of manager who spoke reasonable English, that he would need to access the adjacent room. The team could not do this until the following day when the guest occupying the room had checked out. I subsequently saw the manager a few times. She never mentioned the air conditioner but it never dripped again.

The unseasonably hot weather of the previous few days finally abated. Not by much, but enough to make venturing outside less of a challenge.

. . .

Having told myself I would not complain about the heat, after getting colder and colder in Europe, I had to admit, at least to myself, I was finding it unpleasant. The high today was forecast to be a mere 32°C, positively nippy. We went to a coffee shop we had heard about situated on the 55th floor of the Embassy Tower, in the area of Chong Nonsi. It offered views of a building called Mahanakhon Tower, itself a sight to behold. The design of Mahanakhon is such that it looks unfinished with exposed brickwork and large chunks missing. We found the Embassy Tower complex easily enough, but had some difficulties accessing the elevator. It was located in a secret place. We asked a young local chap for help. Embassy Tower actually consisted of five buildings. Towers 1 - 3 were office space which we could not access. Tower 4 didn't appear to exist at all, future expansion perhaps? Tower 5 was where the coffee shop was perched. To access it one had to find a special door which led to an oddly unnecessary ante-room and finally a lift which went up to level 55. We entered the ante-room, which was quite dark, not realising, that we had to walk through it and out of the other side to get to the lift. Uniformed assistants were everywhere, pointing at things and smiling. It was another very Thai experience.

We emerged from the lift into an area where everything was white; the decor, the coffee-making equipment, the staff were all dressed in white. T said it reminded her of the people in the movie Gattaca. I wondered if we had, finally and, in my case at least, undeservedly, gone to heaven.

. . .

It did have great views and we admired them for a while. T made a short video. The coffee was OK but expensive. We counteracted this expense later in the day by visiting one of my favourite places, in the Ploenchit area of the city. Here, not only is a cappuccino 45 baht, around A$2, as opposed to 130, but they also happily let me order in Thai. In the evening in search of simple sustenance we went to IKEA. Their meatballs had always been a favourite of ours. The store was a relatively new addition in central Bangkok although they had had a store out in the suburbs for a while.

We took an early morning walk through Lumphini Park. Then the MRT to Hua Lamphong. This used to be Bangkok's main train station, until Apiwat opened last year. Now, only a few local trains operate from here. It was very quiet with a few old trains on show, it's more of a museum now.

I thought back fondly, to the times I had taken a train from here to some other part of the country. I remembered the time, just after T and I had arrived in Bangkok. We were keen to explore and were heading for Hua Hin, a resort town a few hours south of the city. Our train was due to depart at 08:05am but, as we stood sweating in the early morning heat, an announcement was made that the train was delayed by 25 minutes. We looked at each other and agreeing another 25 minutes, standing in the heat, was not for us we went home! I regret it looking back of course, but we did eventually make it to Hua Hin. Another fond memory was of the time I'd returned to

Bangkok after a bicycle trip. The day before I'd been swimming in the ocean off the coast near Chumphon, where my friend had a house. Then I'd taken the overnight train, along with my bike, back into the city. Arriving at 06:30am I'd collected my bike from the friendly guys in the cargo hold, pushed it along the platform, feeling like a real explorer, and then cycled the five kilometres or so in the early morning Bangkok traffic back to my apartment. There I'd showered and changed, ready to be at my desk in a modern air-conditioned office by 08:30am. What an adventure.

# In On Nut

The previous day we had changed locations and were renting an apartment in an area of the city, a bit further out of town. It was a nice apartment but our first impressions of the area were not great. There was a small shopping centre nearby but the nearest supermarket was a good 15-minute walk. Too far in the heat. We had something to eat locally and called it a day. The next day T did not feel well. She had a bad cough and a sore throat. She took a COVID test which was negative. I explored the local area alone. There was a small zoo nearby which I found quaint. It was designed for children and had goats, a few sheep and chickens. There were also a number of cafés and an ice-cream shop. It was a great place for an early morning walk. It also seemed to be a popular spot to walk your dog. I often saw dog walkers there, with pocketsful of small plastic bags, clutching the leads of four or five dogs. The recent fad of anthropomorphising animals, particularly dogs, is a strange one. I have friends who constantly refer to themselves as Mum and Dad, when talking about their recently purchased hound. Some neighbours have a dog which can't be left at home alone. Really, what is the point? As a kid I loved having a dog. Of course, I just played with him and did not have to worry about his upkeep or health. I'd take him for walks now and then, but back in the glorious 70s, you'd just let your pooch do its business on the street, or in the park and leave it there. No bending down with little plastic bags and gloves to collect its excrement in those halcyon days.

The next day started with another walk in the small nearby park. I forgot to wear my Fitbit and felt frustrated that my steps would not be counted. How dependent have we become on technology? Many people decry the use of mobile phones at all times and I tend to agree with them. In my early travelling days, on the road in India, I would not have met anywhere near as many people as I did, had my nose been constantly stuck in my phone. Back then, travelling alone, chance encounters were a wonderful thing. I don't imagine they happen much nowadays.

Later, with T still unable to venture far, I went out alone, to do a bit of vital food shopping. On the way back, to avoid just getting home and laying on the bed watching videos, I stopped off at a small restaurant for a drink. It was a pleasant spot, playing music I approved of. I had two beers, and something to eat. The place had one of the biggest fans I've ever seen. I sat enjoying the cool breeze it provided observing my fellow drinkers and diners. They were an eclectic bunch. An oafish looking European fellow was sitting at a nearby table. He took photos of all the dishes he'd ordered, and there were many. As he ate and drank, his complexion went through various stages of pink, to red, to puce and finally to a dangerous shade of crimson. I left before the ambulance was called.

T was beginning to feel a little better. She was due to fly home and had steeled herself for the journey. She did some packing before we went to the coffee shop across the road. The outside air was still full of fumes and we did not want to venture far. There was a large group of excitable locals in one corner, having a shouting competition. It reminded me of when we lived in France and would play tennis on Sunday mornings. The tennis was followed by lunch with, it being France, copious amounts of wine. Usually we would sit outside, but, on colder or wet days, we had to stay indoors. When the weather necessitated this, the owner seated us in a kind of conservatory, with a glass roof and windows.

Conversation in this noisy environment was difficult, for me at least. Most of the others just increased the volume to be heard. Some weeks I wondered that the glass did not shatter.

T flew home in the evening. I watched her taxi leave for the airport and went back inside the apartment, keen to escape the heat and worse, the smog which was covering the city.

# Out of the City for a Day

I left the smoggy city for a day to visit Chris at his guesthouse an hour or so away. I say an hour, but two factors combined to make me a liar. Firstly, I hadn't appreciated that I was now staying on the other side of Bangkok to where he lived. Secondly, I made the mistake of leaving just after 08:00am. The taxi I'd booked crawled through the Bangkok suburbs. At one particular traffic light, I swear we waited five minutes before it turned green. As we circumnavigated the sprawling and congested suburbs, I vowed to find a better option for the way home.

The main reason for the trip out of town, was that some friends were staying at Chris's place. They were convening there before a bike trip, Chris had organised, in Vietnam a few days later. I was unable to join them for various reasons; some logistical, some medical.

. . .

I had a pleasant day with everyone. We went for lunch at a new restaurant, just across the road from the guesthouse. The food was good, but seating was only available at wooden stools, and I soon found my back starting to ache. This problem had begun, earlier in the day, on the lengthy ride in the taxi, but sitting on a stool, with no back support, only exacerbated my agony.

After lunch, and a couple of pain killers, I returned to Bangkok. The journey back into the city was far more pleasant. A taxi took me to Lak Song, now the extent of Bangkok's ever expanding MRT system. Here I boarded a comfortable, and more importantly, cool, train for my journey across the city.

# Bangkok Smiles

I arranged to meet up with my old Bangkok work team. I went to the office in a new tower block in the city. Waiting for everybody to congregate, I sat in the lunch room. Various people I had worked with over the years kept appearing to say hello, which I enjoyed. I also enjoyed the fact that they all said I had not changed a bit. I assured them that, while I might appear the same on the outside, there were a few internal functions that were different. They just smiled.

Later, as we had lunch, for reasons that escape me, the conversation turned to children. One member of the team had been pregnant when we employed her and told me her son was now 10 years old. I remarked that he must have changed a bit. She just smiled.

# A Positive Day

Two things impressed me today. I did some shopping at 7-Eleven, the ubiquitous convenience store, which has branches, many hundreds, even thousands, all over Thailand. I Googled it, over 13000! The staff are generally young, but enthusiastic. Always eager to give you a plastic spoon for your yoghurt, or a plastic fork for your noodles. The young chap who checked my items today was particularly keen. I had taken my own bag, to try and cut back on wastage and he happily took it from me to start packing the various items I had purchased. I watched as he held his little scanner in front of each one - no entering prices these days, it's all on the barcode. Then he carefully, with a good deal of reverence, placed the item in my bag. He had a system. Water first, obviously the heaviest item. This was followed by a couple of pre-packaged noodle dishes, then the cereal packs and finally, as they were of course, the most fragile, the four small pots of yoghurt. Finally, he slid the perfectly packed canvas bag back across the counter to me, with a smile.

-*Well done, good job*, I said, as he continued smiling.

Watching him, I thought that, were I any kind of business owner, I would give this guy a job on the spot. He took such pride in his menial task that surely, with the proper training, which I of course would provide, he could do almost anything.

After the positive shopping experience, I went for a coffee at a new place I'd seen. It was just after 10:00am and I guess they had only just opened because it was still hot inside. The air conditioning was on and would soon do its magic. I ordered my standard *cappo rawn* - hot cappuccino and took a seat. The coffee was delicious. One of the best I had ever had, and certainly in the last few days. I vowed to call in again but next time would wait a while so it was less muggy inside. As I left, I thanked the owner and mentioned the coffee. She seemed happy with my comments and I knew it had been worth getting out of bed that morning.

The next morning, as planned, I had coffee at the same place. This time the experience was even better as, after confirming that I was intending to drink my coffee on site, it arrived, not in a paper cup, but in a large china mug. It was as delicious as the day before.

## A Positive Day

I returned home in the heat. The last few days of my trip were starting to drag. I guess a prisoner feels a bit like this, as he reaches the end of his sentence.

On my early morning walks I thought about odd things. The books I should have kept, the CDs I wished I'd not given away.

When we had moved from France to Australia, as we were paying for the move ourselves, we had been ruthless and, along with recently unworn clothes and infrequently used kitchen items, I had given away all of my books and music. I've since repurchased a few of the CDs, even though I already had the music saved on a hard drive. Books aren't the same. They carry their memories on the covers, not just in the words. I remembered one of the first books I'd bought, Jean-Paul Sartre's Nausea. It cost 50 pence. I'd sit on the train on my daily commute, reading it proudly, assuming everyone around me would be impressed.

The day before my departure dawned. I made two trips to the gym in the building complex. As much to give me something to do, as to keep my daily step count up. It was still hot outside but the smog had lifted slightly and breathing was less unpleasant. I packed my bags, happy to find the numerous T-shirts I'd bought fitted with no problem. I deduced that this was due my having worked my way through most of the pills and potions I'd bought with me four months previously when I set out.

# Time to Go

If the last few days of the trip had hung heavy, the last few hours hung even heavier. I spent more time in the gym, I watched old Star Trek episodes and listened to old Bruce Springsteen concerts I'd seen and heard many times before. Occasionally I did some writing.

I ventured out just once, to my favourite local coffee shop. I'd been there three days in a row and was happy they recognised me and knew what I would order. Should I tell them of my impending departure, in case they wondered why I stopped going in to their lovely shop? It seemed presumptuous, so I said nothing. Maybe, for the next day or two, they would say to each other,
 -*Where's that miserable looking guy who normally comes in about now and orders in a funny accent?*

I could only hope.

## Time to Go

. . .

Finally, I could sit around in the apartment no longer. I called Grab, expecting a wait of a few minutes, but the driver was outside in an instant. We sped along the highway, arriving at the airport in less than 20 minutes. So early that check-in for my flight wasn't even open. Once the process began, I queued and smiled and queued and smiled some more. I panicked slightly when, checking my passport, I could not locate an entry stamp for when I had returned to Thailand from Vietnam. If it were missing, it meant that my passport would show I had overstayed the 30 days allowed in Thailand and be fined, or worse.

-*Perhaps I used the UK passport*, I thought.

I checked and it wasn't there either. When I passed through immigration, there was no issue, so I supposed one of the illegible squiggles on the previous entry stamp somehow made a new one unnecessary. As I sat waiting for my plane, I found the missing entry and exit stamps on another page of my passport.

Waiting for my connection in Singapore, I found a quiet spot, or thought I had. Every time I sat down somewhere, somebody with a small child would sit nearby and I'd be forced to move.

The flight was delayed. These things happen, but it was already a late departure. Eventually, at around 01:30am we took off and headed south. It was the bumpiest flight I have ever been on. The turbulence was caused by converging jet streams over the Australian landmass. For a good part of the journey, my extra legroom seat was restricted by the fact that the cabin crew had to spend most of the flight seated in their little seats, taking up what should have been more legroom for me.

# Isn't it Nice to be Home Again?

We eventually cleared the battling jet streams and arrived safely in Brisbane. It was good to breath the clean air of Australia. As I waited for my bags, I had to smile at the, oh so Australian accent, of the announcements over the Tannoy. At least I could understand them. Arriving in Australia must be a daunting prospect for the first-time entrant to this island nation. Just before landing, a film had been played explaining the illegality of bringing any kind of nut, seed or soil into the country. This had caused some consternation for the Thai/Australian couple seated behind me. Shayne, (he looked, and, more importantly, sounded like a Shayne) was completing both his and his Thai wife's customs form. As he did so he made various acerbic comments, each less amusing than the last. Finally, he checked what foodstuffs she may have bought with her.

-*10 bags of nuts?* he said incredulously. *They won't like that.*

. . .

We deplaned and trooped towards immigration. It's all automated now. For those with the correct documentation anyway. Passport on a scanner; glasses, hat and mask off. A slip of paper slides out of a machine. Take the slip and get the barcode read by another machine. If everything's in order you're in - *welcome to Australia*, says no-one. A few border guards stand idly around, presumably in case of any errant, unwelcome aliens. What takes a bit longer is customs. Here one's completed, rust coloured, slip of paper is quickly inspected by a uniformed customs official.

-*Any alcohol or cigarettes?* he asked while checking the form.


I shook my head and wondered how the nut couple had fared.


I'd booked an Uber to pick me up from the airport but there was no sign of it. I waited 10 minutes or so and took a normal taxi. The driver employed the accelerate, brake, style of driving which added to my nausea from the bumpy flight.


It was a strange feeling entering my apartment after so long away. Familiar but, at the same time, not.


Back in the land of the leg tattoo, it occurred to me that, perhaps the best part of being away, was the couple of days just after you return. Sorting through the clothes and other items you have been using while away and reacquainting yourself with those you have missed.

The shoes I had worn every day, were showing signs of wear. Holes had appeared in both of them. I took them back to the place of purchase and was very happy to be given a new pair in exchange. I didn't tell them I had been wearing the shoes every day for the last four months.

One of the many things I had planned to do when I got back was to go through the various old electrical items; speakers, phones, tablets, iPads etc, that lurked in drawers, long unused. Imagine my delight when I discovered that, during my time away, an electronics recycling centre had opened up just a stone's throw away. A couple of old iPads and iPhones earnt me hundreds of dollars. Conversely, an old Bluetooth speaker I had had for a while, earnt me the princely sum of 60 cents.

I visited one of Brisbane's Sunday market in the Botanic Gardens. It boasts a wide variety of stallholders selling coffee, various types of food, fabrics and skin care products. The first weekend after my return was a wet one but I went anyway. After all, I'd been wandering around cities and towns in Europe, mostly in the rain. Also I was keen to see if anyone had missed me. They hadn't.

The jetlag past. Thursday came around and I met a couple of Brisbane friends with whom I have a standing coffee arrangement.

*-Good trip?* One of them asked.

*-Already planning the next one,* I rakishly responded.

# About the Author

**About Les Stanley**

I was, as Groucho Marx said, born at an early age, in London (England). My parents moved to the Kent coast when I was seven. I caught up with them a year or so later. My school days were unremarkable. Some were marked but usually very badly. The only subject I had any affinity with was English and this was mainly because my parents both spoke it, often at the same time. My career has taken many turns, dips and troughs, a few false starts and even one or two emergency landings.

However, it seems I was destined for an eventual career in the travel industry. Following a failed attempt to make my fortune as a driving instructor, I joined British Airways as a Sales Agent where I stayed for 4 years before emigrating to Australia after marrying local girl Tracy. Fortunately for me this coincided with the rise of the CRS (Computer Reservations System) which later morphed in to GDS (Global Distribution System). I worked in Australia for a company called Galileo and in Europe and Asia for Amadeus. Both companies offered similar products and, obviously, both were best when I was an employee. I retired from the corporate treadmill a few years ago and I'm now officially an author.

My first book was **My Brother's Bicycle**. It

describes a journey of contemplation and misadventure as I attempt, mostly unsuccessfully to re-live a bicycle trip I first embarked on as a fresh-faced 20-year-old More than 40 years ago I headed south with a guy I met at Liverpool Street station in London. Enfield to Athens on a tandem. They said it couldn't be done. For the re-run I was better prepared, or so I thought. But as it turned out it didn't really matter.

My other books have a recurring theme; travel memoirs with a dash of philosophy and healthy cynicism.

# Mostly Fun: Soft Nut Bike Tours of Laos and Thailand

*My fellow adventurers floated towards me on their kayaks in the slow-moving water. I was momentarily tinged with regret for not having joined them. But it was a fleeting moment and I soon realised that, with a life full of regrets, this one would not add much to the total.*

This book describes my thoughts and impressions of two bike trips in Asia. It's not all about cycling. We took trains boats and trucks. There was even a day of kayaking.

On, or off the bike, I had time for contemplation of life's rich patent.

# Cannes Encore! Travel in the Time of COVID

Les and Tracy had lived in The South of France from 1997 to 2007 before moving back to Australia via Bangkok.

So, when COVID began to release its grip on the world and airlines were flying again, they ventured out of their quiet sanctuary in Brisbane and boarded a plane bound for Nice.

Twenty-four hours later we were basking in the dappled sunlight of the Cote d'Azur.

But it wasn't all cheap wine and Salad Niçoise. There were inefficient bank managers and other bureaucrats to deal with. Not to mention noise-sensitive neighbours.

Cannes Encore is the story of two, not so intrepid, travellers and their exploits in the tourist traps of France along with excursions to other less travelled parts of Europe.

Partly together, partly apart, Les and Tracy discover the continent; each in their own unique style.

# Soft Nut Bike Tour of Burma

## Soft Nut Bike Tour of Burma

The Soft Nut Bike Tour of Burma was led by our friend Chris. Boundless resourcefulness and a refusal to accept defeat are just two of his many skills. Snapped chains, grinding gears and punctures are fixed in a flash and if it all gets too much for our less than youthful bodies, he'll conjure up a truck or train to get us to the next outpost of civilisation.

This book describes a ten-day tour of the less travelled area of Southern Myanmar. It's called the Soft Nut Tour because there was also a Tough Nut one which required a level of fitness and fortitude which we no longer possessed - if we ever did.

# My Brother's Bicycle

A journey of contemplation and misadventure as I attempt, mostly unsuccessfully, to re-live a bicycle trip I first embarked on as a fresh-faced 20-year-old.

More than 40 years ago I headed south with a guy I met at Liverpool Street station in London.

Enfield to Athens on a tandem. They said it couldn't be done.

For the re-run I was better prepared, or so I thought. But as it turned out it didn't really matter.

My Brother's Bicycle is a story of (limited) endurance, survival (over boredom) and indomitable human spirit.

www.lesstanley.com

# Go Away Photos

*Istanbul, One of Many Mosques*

*Pudding Shop Time*

*The Glistening Streets of Kuzguncuk*

*Ceauşescu's Folly*

*My 5 Favourite Romanian Items*

*Just Another Romanian Restaurant*

## Go Away Photos

*The Hungarian for Station*

*A Busy Sunday Afternoon in Linz, Austria*

*Paris After the Rain*

*Do You Have Any Cheese? Yes Sir, This is a Cheese Shop Sir*

*The Bungalow of Early Sorrows*

*And for You Sir?*

*Antibes, the Classic View*

## Go Away Photos

*Puccini's Record Player*

*The Leaning Tree of Pisa*

*It's a Train on a Ferry*

*T and I in Sorrento*

*Bangkok. So Hot Even the Ferry Driver is Shirtless*

## Go Away Photos

*Is it Shakespeare or Jesus?*

*Hoi Anh, Vietnam. A Town that Knows What to Do With Tourists*

www.ingramcontent.com/pod-product-compliance
Lightning Source LLC
Chambersburg PA
CBHW072149070526
44585CB00015B/1067